Coram Deo

Princeton Theological Monograph Series

K. C. Hanson, Series Editor

Recent titles in the series

John A. Vissers
The Neo-Orthodox Theology of W. W. Bryden

Stephen Finlan and Vladimir Kharlamov, editors
Theōsis:
Deification in Christian Theology

Byron C. Bangert
Consenting to God and Nature:
Toward a Theocentric, Naturalistic, Theological Ethics

Sam Hamstra Jr.
The Reformed Pastor:
Lectures on Pastoral Theology by John Williamson Nevin

Richard Valantasis et al., editors
The Subjective Eye:
Essays in Honor of Margaret R. Miles

Paul O. Ingram, editor
Constructing a Relational Cosmology

David A. Ackerman
Lo, I Tell You a Mystery

Michael G. Cartwright
Practices, Politics, and Performance:
Toward a Communal Hermeneutic for Christian Ethics

Coram Deo
Human Life in the Vision of God

CARYN D. RISWOLD

Pickwick *Publications*
An imprint of *Wipf and Stock Publishers*
199 West 8th Avenue • Eugene OR 97401

CORAM DEO
Human Life in the Vision of God
Princeton Theological Monograph Series 58

Copyright © 2006 Caryn D. Riswold. All rights reserved. Except for brief quotations in critical publications or reviews, no part of this book may be reproduced in any manner without prior written permission from the publisher. Write: Permissions, Wipf & Stock Publishers, 199 W. 8th Ave., Suite 3, Eugene, OR 97401.

Pickwick Publications
A Division of Wipf & Stock Publishers
199 W. 8th Ave., Suite 3
Eugene, OR 97401

ISBN: 1-59752-598-7

Cataloging-in-publication data:

Riswold, Caryn D.
Coram deo : human life in the vision of God / by Caryn D. Riswold.

Eugene, Ore.: Pickwick Publications, 2005
viii + 166 p.; 23 cm.
Princeton Theological Monograph Series ; 58
ISBN 1-59752-598-7

1. Luther, Martin, 1483–1546—Theology. 2. Sacraments—History of doctrines. 3. Process Theology. 4. Feminist Theology. I. Title. II. Series.

BR 333.2 R58 2006

Manufactured in the U.S.A.

Contents

Acknowledgments / vii
Abbreviations / viii
Introduction / 1

1. Solitary Subjectivity to Relational Agency: Philosophical Roots of Theological Anthropology / 11

2. Human Agency and Divine Mutuality: Feminist Theologies and Process Thought / 40

3. *Finitum Capax Infiniti* in Luther's Writings on the Sacraments / 73

4. The Mission of Jesus and the Vision of God: Implications for Christology and Atonement / 104

5. *Hoc est / Hoc facite*: Theology of the Eucharist as Indicative and Imperative / 137

6. Conclusion / 156

Bibliography / 163

Acknowledgments

The material presented here was written as my dissertation at the Lutheran School of Theology at Chicago in 2000. Therefore, it reads much like the dense scholarship of a doctoral student that it is. Publishing it now is a happy result of a relationship with Wipf and Stock, a publisher who understands the value of presenting dissertations to the academic market so that the rigorous work put into them does not languish in the archives, and that the insights they present may spark future scholars in the field. I would like to thank Dr. K. C. Hanson for enabling me to bring back to life this work that remains a significant theological exercise.

Because the work here is the result of a doctoral program, I must thank the faculty advisors who shepherded me through that process and helped the original birth of this work: Dr. Philip Hefner, Dr. Albert "Pete" Pero, Dr. Vitor Westhelle, and Dr. Kurt Hendel. The first shepherds in my academic development also deserve mention here, Dr. Ann Pederson and Dr. Murray Haar were the ones who initially prompted my pursuit of "the questions" that find some answers and more questions here.

Outside academia, my family has never let me forget where I come from and continues to show me the important difference that makes no matter where I may go in the future. My husband Mark Schelske has been a constant companion on the journey that was this dissertation and is now my first book.

Abbreviations

CJT	*Canadian Journal of Theology*
CTM	*Currents in Theology and Mission*
JR	*Journal of Religion*
LQ	*Lutheran Quarterly*
LW	*Luther's Works, American Edition.* 55 vols. Edited by Jaroslav Pelikan and Helmut T. Lehmann. Philadelphia: Fortress [Muhlenberg]; St. Louis: Concordia, 1955–86.

Introduction

*It is risky to live as if the commonwealth of
the living God were present.*

—Beverly Harrison

Questions and Challenges: Problems, Presuppositions, and Commitments

As a new college graduate, I attended a summer consultation on the atonement at my alma mater.[1] Among the presenting participants at the weeklong series of sessions was then Luther Seminary professor Donald Juel and St. Andrews Theological College professor Joanne Carlson Brown. Brown authored the original article charging Christian theology with divine child abuse in a 1992 issue of the journal *Daughters of Sarah*. It was through the plenary lectures and small group discussions of that week that I was absolutely struck with the power of the questions both implied and blatantly stated in Brown's argument, and the stark difference between her position and that of Juel's traditional, conservative Lutheran theology.

That week opened up the series of questions with which I am still wrestling in this book. Unable to find satisfactory "answers" to the questions that will not leave me alone, I am attempting to reframe the issues surrounding the atonement in a way that takes with utmost seriousness the charges made by feminist theologians like Joanne Carlson Brown. I also hope to take seriously my need to not abandon Christian theology, since that would fail to provide any means of transformation for a community and individuals who not only formed me, but who possess the great potential of a liberating message.

---

[1] *"Did Jesus Die for Our Sins?" A Consultation on the Atonement.* The Shalom Center, Augustana College, Sioux Falls, South Dakota, June 1–3, 1993.

These introductory remarks lay bare some things about me that form and shape the project at hand. One thing is the burning nature of some questions about the relationship between God and the human being that are particularly sparked when speaking about the atonement, and that provide entrée into a discussion about sacramental theology. In order to adequately address the issues of atonement and christology, we must understand how it is that we think about the relationship between God and the human being. The way in which we understand and interpret the life and death of Jesus and his role within that relationship then impacts our theology of the sacraments, particularly the eucharist.

Further, the questions continue to confront and be confronted by my inescapable identity as a Lutheran Christian. I use the term "inescapable" because I find myself working from and with theologies and theologians that are unabashedly critical of patriarchal religious doctrine and paternal theological construction, yet I cannot be convinced that the tradition which formed me is irretrievable or irrelevant. My graduate study began at a United Methodist seminary in California, far from the Lutheran college in South Dakota, and despite my conscious and unconscious efforts to separate myself from this theological heritage, I found myself drawn back to Luther as a relevant and provocative source for theological construction. I am seeking to use Luther as one of my sources, but I am working to reinterpret him and offer a more adequate constructive alternative that embodies what is useable in his tradition. I find the potential for a liberating message within Christian theology, and I find a critical theological resource in Luther.

Finally, I retain a hope that my work will make some difference in a world which needs so many things. The urgency of the crises of ecological destruction, cultural battle lines, economic chaos, and a multitude of other things demand that we view human life in the world in a much different manner than church fathers like Luther did. Because I believe that God makes a difference in the world and to the world, I want to fully understand what difference the relationship with God makes in the life of the human being. Within Christian parameters, that desire leads to various avenues of theological study, as this book will examine. The constellation of issues that I have raised will come together in such a way as to hinge on certain problematic issues and to push with hope for a renewed future.

The question from the title: What does it mean to speak of human life in the vision of God? There are a few key elements to this question: We will first need to understand what we are speaking about in terms of the human being—both from some philosophical roots and then within contemporary theological reflection. It is presumed in this book that the human being is in relationship to God, and therefore it will be important to understand how we speak of God. It is further crucial that we examine the nature of the relationship between God and the human being: What is each doing, gaining, being, and giving? The idea of "the vision of God" will be developed here for its potential to make a difference to the way we understand God and the human being in relationship.

This project weaves many threads of theological study together in a way that I trust will be both its burden and its gift. It seeks to understand the significance of some philosophical and theological resources that undergird much of Christian thought, and to push toward creative appropriation of those traditions in light of some particular contemporary commitments. There is a problem, and there is a commitment as spelled out below. There are resources and there are new paths to forge. There is an argument to be made that requires careful step by step consideration.

The Problem and the Commitment

A commitment to feminist theological criticism grounds what I identify to be the problem of atonement as it presumes and presents an understanding of the relationship between God and the human being, and establishes the basis for a theology of the eucharist. The problem lies squarely within theories of atonement: "We must do away with the atonement, this idea of a blood sin upon the whole human race which can be washed away only by the blood of the lamb."[2] The problem identified in this critical statement is the connection of the suffering and death of Jesus with the redemption of the human race, and the way in which atonement theory lifts up these events as definitive for the relationship between God and the human being, while the sacrament of the eucharist celebrates these events as salvific. This is a result of the prevalence of sacrificial atonement theory for western Christian theology. The problem is connected to the contention that suffering is at least tacitly sanctioned when it is theologically held to be the avenue toward right-relationship with God, if not encouraged as model behavior. Therefore, suffering can become an acceptable, even glorious fact in human life.

This problem grows deeper and more complex when we acknowledge that what we say about the life and death of Jesus is directly connected to what we say about the sacrament of the eucharist. Because of their interrelatedness, theological reflection upon each affects the perspective of the other. Fundamentally, what we say about the relationship between God and the human being is manifest in both of these moments - the life and death of Jesus

---

[2] Joanne Carlson Brown and Rebecca Parker, "For God So Loved the World?" in *Christianity, Patriarchy, and Abuse: A Feminist Critique*, edited by Joanne Carlson Brown and Carole R. Bohn (Cleveland: Pilgrim, 1989) 26.

and the sacraments of the church. It is for this reason that this book seeks to address the theological criticism of atonement through a re-evaluation of the relationship between God and the human being. Rather than focus on reinterpreting atonement *per se*, we will use resources from theological anthropology and sacramental theology to discern a more appropriate way to think about the events of "the Jesus story."

The story leads directly into theological reflection on the sacraments, and it leads to a companion set of problematic issues: The insistence upon the "Real Presence" of Christ in the bread and wine of the eucharist is central in Martin Luther's writings, and this insistence clearly states that the physical body and blood of Christ are present in the sacrament. Luther's writings on the sacraments highlight critical elements of his theology, and indicate a crucial moment in the development of Christianity. Building upon critical reflection on the atonement, we can problematize the sacrament of the eucharist as a ritual participation in the suffering and death of Jesus, a celebration of a tragic death, and/or a tacit approval of the methods by which redemption was brought about. The critical contention underlying these problems is that we live in an abusive society which glorifies suffering, in that it is theologically justified by classical atonement theories and is termed "divine child abuse."[3] This charge will be attended to in this study.

Presuppositions and Assumptions

Grounding this theological reflection are some assumptions about the world and the reality of evil within it. While not a direct part of the constellation of issues in this book, theodicy influences the way in which I will approach them. The "tragic view" of the world and a tendency toward "protest" theodicy informs this work in a significant way:

> Sin and suffering testify to a fundamental cleavage and brokenness that is at the heart of human life. The screams of children and the silence of despair cannot be drowned out by theodicies or justified by the cosmic wonder of nature. *Even the death of a Messiah cannot atone for the anguish of the world.*[4]

This view takes with utmost seriousness the brokenness of the world, and does not allow explanation to be given for it. While I consider this project to be genuinely influenced by hope and optimism, this tangible sense of evil as a part of the nature of the world remains palpable. The understanding of

---

[3] Ibid.
[4] Wendy Farley, *Tragic Vision and Divine Compassion: A Contemporary Theodicy* (Louisville: Westminster John Knox, 1990) 63.

tragedy that accompanies this "retains the sharp edge of anger at the unfairness and destructiveness of suffering." It also is "driven by a desire for justice ...."[5] The twin driving forces of anger and passion for justice come to light throughout this study: anger at a world which demanded the death of Jesus, and passion that seeks transformation of the same forces that continue to destroy lives.

This prevalence of violent imagery and theologically justified suffering within Christianity and some of its dominant atonement theories ought to be unacceptable to anyone committed to the well-being of the planet, and is particularly problematic to feminist theologians. Feminist theology takes as a general presupposition the need for liberation from oppression, particularly the liberation of women, and even more specifically, liberation from violence against women perpetuated by an abusive culture. This is a presupposed commitment of this proposal. The commitment is both to be honest about the reality of suffering and violence, and to seek theologies that move us toward health and wholeness in all dimensions of human life.

> Any attempt to transform a social system without addressing both its spirituality and its outer forms is doomed to failure. Only by confronting the spirituality of an institution and its concretions can the total entity be transformed . . . .[6]

A tangential presupposition of this project is that God works for justice, and is committed to the well-being of the world. Transformation from a state of dis-ease, the state which is the problem, requires confronting the "spirituality" and the "concretions" of Christianity. Theology as well as religious practice ought to serve the liberating vision of God and express a relationship between the human being and God which emphasizes those liberating and humanizing aspects. What *does* it mean for us to live as a human being in the vision/presence of God?

Underlying the statements about problems in Western Christian theology are general assumptions about what it means to be human, and what it means for the human being to live in relationship with God. Reflection on theological anthropology has a rich and detailed history in itself. For purposes of this project, we will remain committed to these questions: What does it mean to be human? What does it mean for God to be God? What does it mean for the human being and God to be in relationship? Characteristics of the relationship between God and the human being are at least presupposed, and usually asserted in any conversation about atonement theory or sacra-

---

[5] Ibid., 13.
[6] Walter Wink. *Engaging the Powers: Discernment and Resistance in a World of Domination* (Minneapolis: Fortress, 1992) 10.

mental theology. For this reason, we must establish a basis for talking about the relationship before we can attend to the problematics in sacramental theology or atonement theory.

A proposal will arise from the synthesis of these problems, presuppositions, and commitments. This proposal will suggest that whatever it is we say about God and the human being and the relationship between them is fundamental to reinterpreting atonement theory, which is manifest in the sacraments, and ultimately relevant to human life as it is lived in the context of a messy and complicated world.

Thesis Statement

Theology needs a new understanding of theological anthropology that effectively intertwines traditional resources and contemporary constructions in order to solve the problem identified with atonement theories and sacramental theology. The solutions that I will propose here depend upon a renewed concept of theological anthropology, as the relationship between God and the human being, which will present two mutually participating, enhancing partners, each with an ability to make a difference in the life of the other. This enables a re-examination of the life and death of Jesus in a way which fosters a new understanding of the eucharist as an embodied commitment to struggle, a willingness to risk for justice, and a desire to fulfill the vision of God as truth, beauty, and goodness.

Parameters and Structure

While the thesis statement above begins with atonement theories as problematic, this book is not "about" atonement. It does not exhaustively review the history of atonement theory and it does not present a new theory for understanding atonement. This study suggests that a return to the fundamental way in which we understand the relationship between God and the human being allows us to address the problems noted above. This is because atonement is fundamentally about the relationship between God and the human being. In proposing some solutions to the problems identified with atonement theory, the book will move to examine the difference such reinterpretation makes for the theology of the eucharist. The relationship between God and the human being is the basis from which we speak of christology and atonement, and our understanding of these things inevitably affects our understanding of the sacrament of eucharist.

In this project, theological anthropology will be understood as the study of the relationship between God and the human being—the dynamics of that relationship, as well as the characteristics of each member of the relationship.

It will not focus specifically on traditional anthropological concepts like sin and justification. I believe this shift in focus to be an appropriate approach to a theological problem in atonement identified specifically by feminism, utilizing the feminist emphasis on experience to determine an adequate solution. By centering the discussion on the anthropological, specifically the relational issues between God and the human being, we are enabled to ascertain a more appropriate sacramental theology as a part of human life.

A theology of the sacraments plays a significant role in this study, as a beneficiary of theological anthropology and atonement theory and christology. Sacramental theology (the phrase used here synonymously with theological reflection on the sacraments) will not be examined for its broad range of issues and its deep heritage within Christian interpretations, but will serve as exemplary of a moment of Christian expression. It is one of those concretions of spirituality and theology which will be examined as it reflects and presents an understanding of the relationship between God and the human being.

A Word on Method

Method is tied to commitment. As previously stated, the commitment underlying this project lies in feminist theology and its focus on the liberation of humanity from the cultural evils of sexism, racism, and poverty.[7] The means by which this project will unfold addresses that consideration. The project begins with a stated problem, suggests a solution for that problem, and then demonstrates the steps by which the problem can be solved. To do theology from a feminist perspective demands that one pay serious attention to the theological tradition which is identified as problematic. For this project, that is exemplified partially in Luther's writings on the sacraments, and partially in some theories of atonement. It also demands that one present one's own argument in a substantiated manner, and if need be, describing some sort of relationship between tradition and contemporary proposals. This relationship may be either contradictory, synthesized, or harmonious. This study moves from roots in traditional philosophical discourse, to analysis of contemporary options, to a critical exploration of traditional resources using insights gained within the contemporary realm, and then on toward constructive proposals that address the initially stated problem. The contemporary options found here in feminist and process theologies are used as tools to evaluate the applicability of the traditional resources found specifically in Luther, and Luther stands as a critical traditional voice holding contemporary theological

---

[7] The notion of cultural evil, for this project, comes from Nel Noddings: Cultural evil is "our way of organizing and institutionalizing pain"; *Women and Evil* (Berkeley: University of California Press, 1989) 142.

proposals accountable. The rendering of a constructive proposal, therefore, depends upon an appropriate synthesis of the two.

As I stated earlier, the many things which this project brings together can be both its gift and its burden. There is a constellation of issues which are unique and yet interrelated. The challenge will be for me to describe the picture that emerges when all of the correct "stars" are viewed together. If this is a methodology of eclecticism, then it is important to be careful and responsible with the relationship to each component, and to detail the ways in which each "star" relates to the others. In viewing a constellation, one cannot see "the whole picture" without seeing all or at least most of the parts. The sacraments, God and the human being, the atonement, Jesus Christ, and even some underlying thoughts about theodicy and justice in God's terms and the world's reality—all of these things are important to theology, and this book carefully brings them together.

The Steps

In order to discern the shape of the constellation, the way in which the various issues of this book come together to present a picture, we must see the way in which they relate to one another. As I have stated, the central driving issue of the project lies within the feminist theological criticism of atonement theory. By way of offering a solution to these problems, I will offer a reconstruction of our understanding of the relationship between God and the human being. Altering how we view that relationship fundamentally alters how we view the events of atonement and christology. With this being done, we finally turn to the implications such shifts have for a theology of the eucharist as a public Christian expression of faith: the expression of our relationship with God.

First, we will explore the philosophical "turn to the subject," which brought about theological anthropology as an intellectual or academic discipline. Immanuel Kant's writing provides resource for this discussion because it establishes a philosophical basis for speaking about the human being as independent subject. But there arises a need to move beyond his understanding, and we will see a proposal for a "turn to the agent," which is embodied in several contemporary theological texts. The move back to some philosophical roots of anthropology as a theological discipline allows us to draw out some themes that continue to be of importance, and themes that will reappear throughout the book. These roots will extend to contemporary notions that propose the specific challenge of a "turn to the agent" and its implications for contemporary theology. This exploration firmly establishes a means for speaking about the human being in the world.

Second, I will look specifically at feminist and process theologies and the ways in which some theologians within in these schools of thought address a concept of the human being and her relationship with God. Select readings and proposals will lift up the particular ways in which contemporary "feminist" and process theologians speak about the human being, about God, and about their relationship. A particular way of speaking about experience influences each of these ways of doing theology, and the connections between scholars in these two schools of thought create a conversation that stresses similar themes. They will provide resource for construction and criticism in a return to the problematic issues driving the study.

Third, the sacramental theology of Luther and its implications for this discussion of the relationship between the human being and God will be critically examined as a ground for new construction and old resource. As an integral part of the history of Christian reflection on the themes of the sacraments and the relationship between God and the human being, Luther serves as a sort of grounding point for this project, and his writings on the sacraments provide the central means with which we will address the treasure and the trouble of his reflection on the relationship between God and the human being. We will see how the contemporary theological proposals examined previously can be used as interpretive tools for reading Luther in the context of a new millennium, both drawing from his theology and exposing its inadequacies. Luther in turn will serve as a theological challenge to the anthropocentric tendencies of the contemporary theologians selected here.

Fourth, I will show how a renewed understanding of the relationship between God and the human being both enables and necessitates a fresh interpretation of the life and death of Jesus, and criticism of atonement theory in general. This approach to the problems presents some of the history of atonement theory, discerns some themes of atonement, and criticizes them from the perspectives detailed in previous chapters. This step is important as it both returns us to the initial problem stated above, and as it propels us to think about sacramental theology as an expression of a crucial aspect of Christian life: the relationship between God and the human being.

Finally, a constructive proposal for a theology of the eucharist will be offered, incorporating theological anthropology and criticism of atonement and christology in such a way as to address the critical problem of the eucharist and to create space for reinterpreting the sacrament. We will see how concepts of the human being, God, and Jesus Christ as re-envisioned in this project, suggest a theology of the eucharist which is both indicative and imperative in terms of human life in the vision of God. The eucharist makes a statement about the reality of the world, and it makes a statement about

God's hope for the world. Our participation in it signifies our commitment, our willingness to risk, and God's unfailing presence with the world.

1

Solitary Subjectivity to Relational Agency:
Philosophical Roots of Theological Anthropology

Theological Anthropology: Introductory Comments

"THEOLOGICAL anthropology may be able to deal with persons in their genuine concreteness only by a second 'turn,' from the person as patient or subject of consciousness to the person as agent."[1] This challenge is the impetus for this chapter. The rest of this study builds upon this suggestion of agency as a second "turn" in speaking about humanity. This suggestion, however, presupposes what is called the first philosophical "turn": the turn toward the subject.

This is why the first steps in this project move us back to the realm of Enlightenment philosophy. A central concern of this book is to illumine the relationship between God and the human being as a means to answer some theological questions raised by atonement theory. In order to get into the conversation about the relationship between God and the human being, we must understand the philosophical origins for speaking about the human being *per se*, and then move toward speaking about the relationship of the human with the divine. This chapter first moves back to explore the roots of language about the human being in terms of its vocabulary found in the philosophy of Immanuel Kant. The point of this is not to provide an exhaustive search into Kant's philosophy, but to establish the root of theological conversation about

---

[1] David H. Kelsey, "The Human Being," in *Christian Theology: An Introduction to Its Traditions and Tasks,* eds. Peter C. Hodgson and Robert H. King (Philadelphia: Fortress, 1982, 1985) 192.

the human being in the philosophical shift toward speaking about the human as subject. From this basis we will move on to develop an understanding of the human as agent in relationship to God and the world.

> The term 'anthropology' first entered into common use in the sixteenth century as the name for a subordinate discipline within metaphysical psychology.... Then, 'anthropology' came to refer specifically to human psychology. This made it possible for the doctrine on the nature of the human being to be removed from its earlier metaphysical setting and made independent.[2]

The independence of anthropology as a discipline characterizes the modern philosophical and theological era. The suggestion that we can and ought to speak of human beings as subjects, as beings with experience worth examining and understanding at a deep level, critically shifts the direction of philosophy and theology. In this study, I follow Pannenberg's view that it becomes essential for human beings to speak of "themselves in relation to the world only if they presupposed God as the common author of both themselves and the world."[3] Consequently, after I establish the independence of the human being as subject with the philosophical resources of Kant's Enlightenment thought, I move on to examine the relationship of the independent being with God, and the implications of that for her relationship to the world. The concept of "relationship" is a crucial for this project, and will be developed in a number of ways. The fundamental nature of the relationship of the human being to God makes it the focus of theological anthropology as it is used in this project. This relationship founds the existence of the human being, and it establishes her relationship to the world.

"With the modern era's attention to the human subject, theological anthropology has come into its own as a distinct theological topic."[4] From this statement, the *Dictionary of Feminist Theologies* goes on to suggest that attention to the human subject finds a distinct articulation in feminist theology. Theological anthropology is a prominent concern of two leading schools of contemporary thought: feminist theology and process thought.[5] These

---

[2] Wolfhart Pannenberg, *Anthropology in Theological Perspective*, trans. Matthew J. O'Connell (Philadelphia: Westminster, 1985) 16.

[3] Ibid., 11.

[4] "Anthropology, Theological," in *Dictionary of Feminist Theologies*, ed. Letty M. Russell and J. Shannon Clarkson (Louisville: Westminster John Knox, 1996) 10.

[5] Process theology is a term used to identify those theologians working out of the philosophy of Alfred North Whitehead, and the interpretation and development of it by Charles Hartshorne. Theologians often align themselves with either Whitehead or Hartshorne. For purposes of this project, I identify with process theology as arising out of Whitehead, and rely mainly on my own reading of his texts. Other theological interpretations will function in relationship

schools of thought inform this book as both critical tools and constructive resources, and their questioning what it means to be human, in relationship to the world and to God, provides an impetus for the study at hand.

We will return to a consideration of these schools of thought after briefly introducing the origin of some issues in speaking about the human being. The origin lies in part within particular vocabulary, terms, and concepts arising from the philosophical Enlightenment of the late eighteenth and early nineteenth centuries, found here in Kant's writing. The point of this exploration is to tease out some of the key issues regarding the conversation about being human in order to see the shift through which they have moved from philosophical origination to contemporary theological manifestation. In eliciting some origins in philosophical anthropology, we can discover some fundamental concerns for the human being that are picked up as they are expressed and enhanced in feminist and process theologies.

Why begin the conversation with reference to the Enlightenment? We will see in the following sections how particular concepts and terms from Kant's philosophy prove indispensable for any conversation about the human being as subject. As these are the roots for our modern conversation about human subjectivity, it is important to understand the ways they originated and continue to function. These terms and concepts are then used to set an agenda for theological conversation about the human being in relationship to God. We will move from Kant to some contemporary thinkers and their proposals for understanding human beings, their subjectivity and their agency. We will see how each draws conceptually from terminology found in Kant, enhancing and questioning its traditional philosophical meaning.

Origins/Definitions:
Kant and the Enlightenment

While this project seeks to articulate and work with a *theological* anthropology, we gain from Kantian *philosophical* principles, several specific terms and concepts that inform the conversation: they include autonomy, reason, the human will, the categorical imperative, and freedom of decision. On the one hand, these concepts are often presupposed in contemporary conversations about theological anthropology, and come to be used in new ways, while on the other hand, they inform the proposal of this chapter explicitly. Consequently, I will explore Kant's thinking as an entrée to what follows.

---

to this.

Autonomy

Autonomy characterizes the human as she is able to make her own laws, literally—*auto nomos*—to be governed by her own law. Kant states what becomes a motto of the Enlightenment, *Sapere aude!* (dare to know! know boldly!), in decrying the faults of the human condition in the modern era. "Laziness and cowardice are the reasons why so great a portion of mankind, after nature has long since discharged them from external direction, nevertheless remain under lifelong tutelage."[6] Tutelage is the condition under which the human being remains bound to the direction of and an obligation to others. Autonomy is its corrective. This call for daring knowledge illumines Kant's call to courage: " 'Have courage to use your own reason!'—that is the motto of enlightenment."[7] Decisions made and actions taken on the basis of external necessities or influences like the reason of others are characteristic of an individual under tutelage.

This illuminates in part the distinction between heteronomy and autonomy on which Kant relies. In this distinction, the autonomous will is determined by nothing other than itself, and the heteronomous will is determined by external forces, such as force, coercion, and satisfaction. "The point is that in obeying the moral law for the sake of the law alone, the will is autonomous because it is obeying a law which it imposes on itself: heteronomy occurs whenever the will obeys laws, rules, or injunctions from any other source."[8] Self-determination of the will is crucial to Kant's philosophy, and it involves other aspects of his thought. Governance on the basis of one's own volition is the point to emphasize here. The principle of autonomy "implies that the determining ground of the moral will must be, not any empirical rule or concept, but the formal concept of lawfulness in general, which is a concept of pure reason."[9] That is, it is not a particular rule that one must obey; it is a general notion of moral law itself, and the entire concept of lawfulness, that beg obedience. If one acts out of fear of retribution, or of obedience to the particular letter of a specific law imposed externally, then one acts heteronomously.

Autonomy as freedom of reason is a particular characteristic of the human being in the public realm. Kant distinguishes between freedom in the public and the private realms: Enlightenment is "the freedom to make public

---

[6] Immanuel Kant, "What is Enlightenment?" (1784) trans. Lewis White Beck (Englewood Cliffs: Prentice Hall, 1990) 83.
[7] Ibid.
[8] John Kemp. *The Philosophy of Kant* (London: Oxford, 1968) 60.
[9] Ibid., 61.

use of one's reason at every point."[10] Public freedom is here understood as the ability of each person as thinker or scholar to devise arguments and hold opinions according to her own reason. This includes the ability of the individual to express her thoughts on the justice or injustice of certain laws or practices. However, Kant also speaks of the private use of reason which binds the individual to obey the statutes of the office she is to carry out. "Here argument is certainly not allowed—one must obey."[11] This dichotomy is explained in part by an understanding of the world which holds firmly to the importance of individual freedoms of expression while maintaining the need for structure and order.[12]

Kant's best example of this is the clergyperson who is bound by virtue of office to preach and teach according to the principles of the church body. However, as a scholar and as an individual, the person is allowed and even encouraged to write and speak about personal assessment of the merit and failing of such teachings in the church. The belief here is that a person would not hold an office if she thought the teachings of it were inherently contradictory or wrong, rather that there is believed to be some truth in the teachings themselves. This example leads Kant to offer the example of a church reforming by virtue not of clergy who preach and teach what they wish regardless of the community standards, but by virtue of the collection of scholarly voices who exercise their freedom of reason in individual public ways. In this way, the orders can and will change. This process holds up the importance of both institutional integrity and individual freedoms. The human being is bound to one and free within another.

For our conversation about human subjectivity, governance by a self-generating and sustaining consciousness, not by external concerns or forces, marks a philosophical shift toward subjectivity that proves to be crucial in the development of theological notions. The very notion of independence is grounded here, and its nuances provoke some questions of accountability and relationality. Kant provides resources for answering these questions in his concepts of the human will and the categorical imperative.

---

[10] Kant, "What is Enlightenment?," 84.

[11] Ibid., 85.

[12] This connects nicely with Martin Luther's understanding of freedom as presented in his essay, "The Freedom of a Christian" (1520). The Christian is presented as perfectly free from earning his or her salvation and worth before God, and perfectly dutiful with regard to serving the neighbor in the name of Christ.

Reason

For Kant, reason is that which enables an individual to be autonomous, to confidently make decisions and adopt moral and ethical principles of her own accord, while providing for some universalizable aspect.

> We are bound to confess that human reason contains not only ideas, but ideals, which possess, not, like those of Plato, creative, but certainly practical power—as regulative principles, and form the basis of the perfectibility of certain actions.[13]

The focus here is on the role of reason as a determining factor in human activity. Reason determines human activity exercised by the autonomous self, centered around ideas and ideals, as well as the important concept of duty. Reason supports itself and depends on no other force of justification. Rather than being another heteronomous force, forcing the human will to succumb to its own interests, like civil law or obligation to another, reason is unique: "Rational nature is distinguished from others in that it proposes an end to itself."[14] We will see how the categorical imperative expresses this emphasis on being an "end," but here we note that reason is such that it functions uniquely to form human subjectivity. To be subject to one's own rational will is what constitutes human subjectivity. It is a self-sufficient ground for decision and action. From the guidance offered by our human capacity for reason, we are enabled to live a moral life.

Reason, furthermore, compels human action:

> That reason possesses the faculty of causality, or that at least we are compelled to represent it, is evident from the *imperatives*, which in the sphere of the practical we impose on many of our executive powers. The words *I ought* express a species of necessity . . . .[15]

Kant goes on to further analyze the role of this "ought" within the realm of duty. "The idea of an *ought* or of duty indicates a possible action, the ground of which is pure conception."[16] An ought implies a real possibility grounded in a concept, and it originates purely through reason. Duty is a powerful force in bringing about human action. The need to act according to duty

---

[13] Immanuel Kant, *The Critique of Pure Reason*, trans. J. M. D. Meiklejohn (London: Bell & Sons, 1893) 351.

[14] Kant, "Foundations of the Metaphysics of Morals," (1785) trans. Lewis White Beck (Englewood Cliffs: Prentice Hall, 1990) 54.

[15] *Critique of Pure Reason*, 338.

[16] Ibid., 339.

rests solely on the relation of rational beings to one another, in which the will of a rational being must always be regarded as legislative, for otherwise it could not be thought of as an end in itself.[17]

Kant defines duty in this way: "The objective necessity of an action from obligation is called duty."[18] Pure reason, in this manner, exists in a causal relationship to other things and produces the sense of duty or obligation.

The possibility that reason could be spoken of as a causal force, as it leads a human being to speak in terms of what ought to be and to act accordingly, suggests human experience which has a capacity beyond sheer physical natural embodiedness and its causality. An *ought* has ground in human rational thought processes—a conscious response to the world's state of affairs. This is where the person who is free in the public realm to discuss and express opinions and thoughts about the world can make suggestions for reform. A distinction between practical and theoretical reason addresses both the ethical knowledge and the "ideal standards which are presupposed in much of our thinking . . . ."[19] Human subjectivity, we may say, governs itself by virtue of reason which attends to both practical ethical concerns and ideals which in turn can direct such practicality.

The drive of the *ought* factors significantly into a contemporary theological conversation about the human being and her relationship to the world. Reason is that capacity of the human being as a subject which arises out of her autonomy and compels such action on the basis of the ought. This development of human subjectivity allows us to think about the individual person as capable of particular thought processes and leads us to understand actions as a result of such thought.

Human Will

The human will rises out of this understanding of reason. Reason is a human capacity set apart from other aspects of nature which possess causative power. In this way, the human being can determine her subjective reality by virtue of her own will.

> If reason stands in a causal relation to phenomena, it is a faculty which originates the sensuous condition of an empirical series of effects . . . it

---

[17] "Foundations," 51.

[18] Ibid., 57.

[19] A. C. Ewing. *A Short Commentary on Kant's Critique of Pure Reason* (Chicago: University of Chicago Press, 1938) 200.

is intelligible, and it consequently cannot be subject to any sensuous condition, or to any time-determination by a preceding cause.[20]

Being subject to no other determining factor, therefore, the human being is self-determined when the self is understood to contain and foster the capability of reason. Kant speaks thus of the human will, that force by which decisions can be made in the state of autonomy. "Reason is consequently the permanent condition of all actions of the human will."[21] A human being is conditioned by her will, thus governed by reason, thus governed by herself.

The human will, as another way of speaking about self-determination, is the causal principle, the mechanism through which the human being compels herself to believe or act in particular ways.

> The will is thought of as a faculty of determining itself to action in accordance with the conception of certain laws. Such a faculty can be found only in rational beings. That which serves the will as the objective ground of its self-determination is a purpose, and if it is given by reason alone it must hold alike for all rational beings.[22]

The will dependent upon rationality is a self-determined human will. It is critical for understanding human subjectivity. As a wholly internalized and at the same time universalizable process, self-determination governed by rational human volition ensures that the autonomous subject is accountable to the standards of "reason," some rationally conceived purpose, and that communal morality can develop accordingly when we come to speak about relationality.

Kant's concept of the human will is an expression of his other concepts like autonomy and reason. It is free in that it is bound to no external tutelage for determining itself, and it is bound to the principles of reason. When we understand "the public" as the sphere of individuals freely expressing their ideas and ideals, we grasp the magnitude of human free will. When we understand "the private" as the carrying out of each person's office in the community, his or her vocation, we grasp the importance of obedience to the laws of a stable community. The interface between the two is the way in which community standards come to change and the way mores ebb and flow throughout the lifetime of one individual.

---

[20] *Critique of Pure Reason*, 341.
[21] Ibid., 342.
[22] "Foundations," 44.

Categorical Imperative

The categorical imperative underlies all of the above analysis, is very crucial to Kant's philosophy, and is provocative for contemporary theology. Although Kant suggests that "the real morality of actions . . . is completely unknown to us,"[23] the categorical imperative suggests that the morality of decisions lies in their universal appropriateness, and reflexive effect. The categorical imperative is stated thus: "Act as though the maxim of your action were by your will to become a universal law of nature."[24] An action is determined to be moral when it universally applies to all similar situations, and it is an action that you would consent being applied to you in a similar situation. Human decision has potential ramifications far beyond its own immediacy, and is presented as that which has potential to affect human affairs universally.

The reflexive aspect of this provides us some frame for thinking about justice. Assuming the rationality of the human will, acting in accord with this categorical imperative, we can suppose that each act should be such that any person would consent to its appropriateness.

As Kant uses examples to illumine this principle, so shall we. Let us consider a public decision which raises many issues: The 42nd president of the United States is known to have had extra-marital affairs with various women. At some point in their relationship, his wife decided to stay married to him. Let us assume for the sake of this example that conventional wisdom regarding monogamy in marriage is the norm. The question becomes: Why does she decide to remain married to him? Why does he continue being married to her? She gains politically and professionally by being associated with a man who has succeeded in his professional life, and he gains politically and professionally through her support and reinforcement. Some analysts suggested that her support of him determined the country's support of him throughout public scandal. For her situation, it appears to be the best decision to remain married and publicly committed to her husband.

However, if we apply the categorical imperative to this situation, we find something else. Let us consider her decision alone: Faced with a husband who has extramarital affairs, she chooses to remain married to him. Shall we say that every woman, when faced with a husband who has extramarital affairs, ought to remain in her marriage? Perhaps it is difficult to come to some universalizable action in such a situation, but if we say that *all* women who are married to men who have affairs *ought* to stay with them, the First Lady's decision is obviously flawed. If it were universalized to all other similar situations, it would have detrimental effects for women and for marriages. Women

---

[23] *Critique of Pure Reason*, 341 n.
[24] "Foundations," 38.

would force themselves to remain in situations where they were not respected and possibly even ignored, for the sake of some greater good. Taking this to extreme situations, we can see how easy the logic can apply for wives who are being abused by their husbands, and how difficult it becomes for them to leave even when their survival and well-being depend upon it.

A Kantian principle within the categorical imperative here applied states that human beings are to be thought of and treated as if they are ends in and of themselves, not a means to another end. "Man [sic], however, is not a thing, and thus not something to be used merely as a means; he must always be regarded in all his actions as an end in himself."[25] The autonomous person not only makes her own decisions based on the power of her reason and will, she is an end in and of herself, not to be used as a means to another end. We can see how the situation of this marriage fails to meet this criterion of morality as well. A woman in a marriage with a man who has affairs should not allow herself to be used as a means for the ends of her husband. No person ought to do this. This suggests that the woman in question ought not "put up with" his disrespectful actions.

We could suggest then, that *all* women who are married to men who have affairs *ought not tolerate* his behavior. What this means for each woman in that situation may differ: The woman *ought to divorce* the man; or more generously, The woman *ought to make clear* that if the man has more affairs, *she will divorce* him. Clearly, one's personal moral and ethical standards determine the manner in which she will "not tolerate" his behavior. Our decisions ought to be made in such a way that, in line with the categorical imperative, they are universalizable, and that they are therefore ethically appropriate. If we acted in such a way to use another person as a means to our end, its universal applicability would lead to action that we would not wish inflicted upon ourselves (being treated as means), and that would subsequently foster a human community of distrust and deceit.

We can see how the First Lady acts on heteronomous motives and therefore uses her husband as means to her own political and professional ends, in the same way that the President acts to use her as means to his political success. Consequently, her action (as well as his) does not qualify as a representative of Kant's action motivated by the categorical imperative. Further, if we understand the role of spouse as vocation or office in life, then one is bound to obey the standards of that role, here presumed to include fidelity. The two aspects of the categorical imperative presented here possess tremendous potential for affecting how we think and speak about the human being as subject and eventually as actor. Under the guise of Kant's categorical imperative,

---

[25] Ibid., 46.

all decisions made by the individual have consequences for the moral structure of the human community. This makes the decision of a public figure like the First Lady particularly interesting to analyze. The human being as subject does make her own decisions, however, and lives with its results.

These two principles of the categorical imperative again touch upon the interface between being free and bound. The human being is free to act according to her rational will, but in accord with the maxim that any action shall itself be universalizable so as to be applied to any other member of the community. Likewise, the individual is free to decide for herself, but shall not act in such a way as to use another person as means to her own end. These things constitute a breach of morality or justice within the human community, and are taken seriously by Kant. The centering of the discussion on the human being as subject of her own reason and will is not without connection to standards of ethical behavior in the private and the public spheres.

Freedom to Decide

Kant ultimately believed that freedom operates in all situations and moral decisions. The will, for Kant, is free when it is moral, and it is moral when it is free to decide. The human will is free to decide its actions: "The proposition that the will is a law to itself in all its actions, however, only expresses [the categorical imperative.] Therefore a free will and a will under moral laws are identical."[26] For the human will to be free, for it to be subject to its own governance (autonomous), implies that it will act morally, that is, in such ways that meet the criterion of universalizability.

> The concept of autonomy is inseparably connected with the Idea of freedom, and with the former there is inseparably bound the universal principle of morality, which is the ground in Idea of all actions of rational beings, just as natural law is the ground of all appearances.[27]

Autonomy, freedom, and rationality converge in a human will that, in accord with the categorical imperative, acts morally. Because "the only laws that we can will to be universalized are, according to the fundamental principles of Kant's ethics, the moral laws."[28] The human will acting rationally and independently freely decides according to the laws it imposes upon itself—the universalizable laws of morality and justice.

It is this philosophical and ethical basis that sparks theological re-thinking about the human being, particularly in terms of her relationships in the

---

[26] "Foundations," 64.
[27] Ibid., 70.
[28] *A Short Commentary*, 234.

world. If we insist that the human being is governed by her own sense of lawfulness in such a way that adheres to moral law, what is to become of her activity in the world? What may we say about her relationship to God and to her community? For this book, this is Kant's most important legacy: He provides a language and vocabulary for us to begin thinking about human being and human subjectivity, and he provides resources for constructing the independent human being as subject in the world and as member of the community. The nature of the shift in thinking that this produces is referred to as his "Copernican" revolution: A radical recentering of philosophical discourse on the human being as subject. From here we can move toward theological interpretation of what it means to be a human being.

Moving Forward to Contemporary Reflection

Kantian Resources

Kant's thought is an essential background for contemporary analysis of the human being in relationship to God, because we first must be able to speak of the human being as an individual subject, possessing her own free will, and capable of making decisions and acting on them, before we can examine the ways in which she relates to the world and acts within it. The key philosophical terms we have explored—autonomy, reason, self-determination, freedom, human will—begin with a primary image of a solitary individual self. By focusing on establishing autonomy as characteristic of human individuality, and the decision-making processes that constitute a human will, rationality, and morality, Kant provides a solid base from which we can move toward a contemporary concern for illuminating human agency.

Contemporary conversation about the human being presupposes this explication of subjectivity. The presentation here of some select concepts within Kant's philosophy marks the modern turn toward the human being as subject and as independent actor in the world. This turn is used to illumine the beginning of this study as it establishes the basis for our conversation about the human being. From this basis, we will build upon the philosophical exploration of human subjectivity and move in a theological direction.

By bringing Kant's vocabulary into a contemporary conversation, we can see where his concepts can and will foster a new conversation about relationships—including the external and the public interactions of the human self—and allow us to speak more specifically about human agency. This is where the philosophical meets the theological, and the interplay between Kant's resources and the present concerns of this book begin. We will move to speaking about human agency, and need to establish the parameters within which we will do that.

Agency

Here are two philosophical definitions of "agent," and one common definition of "agency":

> Agent (*ago*, to act), one who, that which, acts.[29]

> Agent: . . . Here it is usually held that to be a moral agent, . . . one must be free and responsible, with a certain maturity, rationality, and sensitivity—which normal adult human beings are taken to have.[30]

> Agency: . . . 7. the state of being in action or of exerting power. 8. a means of exerting power or influence; instrumentality . . . . —Syn. 8. intercession.[31]

For this discussion, we will take the spirit of these statements and not immerse ourselves in the technical nuances of the philosophies which are concerned with the inner workings of human agency and human acting.[32]

For my purposes in this project, agency is understood as the ability of a human being to act in the world. This simple statement presumes several things which must be laid bare: a) the human being is capable of some antecedent decision processes, and that intentionality may play a role, b) the human being is independent in those processes, c) that the human being exists in the world and therefore actions often have consequence because, d) existing in the world entails relationality, therefore, e) ability-to-do entails responsibility-for-it. Through our examination of Kant's philosophy, we have seen how the basis for the presumptions are attained: if we understand the human being as subject, we grant her decision-making ability and the independence of her will. The latter presumptions move us from an image of the human being as solitary subject to that of a relational being, and hence to the

---

[29] William Fleming. *The Vocabulary of Philosophy: Mental, Moral, and Metaphysical* (New York: Sheldon, 1873) 19.

[30] Dagobert D. Runes, ed., *The Dictionary of Philosophy* (New York: Philosophical Library, 1942) 7.

[31] *The Random House College Dictionary, Revised Edition* (New York: Random House, 1988) 25.

[32] See "Choosing, Deciding, and Doing," in *The Encyclopedia of Philosophy*, ed. Paul Edwards (New York, MacMillan Free, 1967) 2:96–104. This provides a thorough and intriguing analysis of the distinctions between choosing, deciding and doing, as levels of conscious and active behavior.

human being as agent. To be in relation is a fundamental characteristic of being human; it necessitates both decision and action, and brings responsibility with it.

This is how we can speak of the human being not only as subject of her own will and reasonable governance, but as capable of acting in the world in such a way that presumes and establishes her relationship to it. Acting in the world presumes relating to the world. The applicability of Kant's "ought" is important here: To look at the world, and say that I ought to do such and such, implies not only that I have the ability to conceive of it and to decide thus, but that I have some ability to do such and such. This brings us to a sort of line defining the human being—the boundary between herself (thought and will) and the rest of the world (relationship and action). This speaks to another legacy with which Kant leaves us, which we may refer to as boundaries of the self. The private self is bound to reason and universal laws and statutes of the office, and the public self is free to act by virtue of her will and reason. The sense of boundary between the two is important for contemporary theology, particularly as we will see in the development of feminist theology and the metaphysics of process thought. It is the move from the moments of solitary subjectivity, across the boundary of the self into the relationality of the world that this analysis hopes to illuminate.

For Kant and for this study of the human being, it is understood that the human subject is continually a social creature who is simultaneously affecting her context and being affected by it. In the examination of the categorical imperative, for example, we see that the environment within which a person makes a decision or takes an action has a great effect on her. The way in which the situation of the individual affects her decision and action is the way in which it in part determines her subjectivity. The relationship between the private person and the public realm leads us to further examine the importance of relationality for this study.

Relationality

To build upon Kant's philosophy and his explication of human subjectivity, we must examine the way that relationships in the world affect being human. Relationality as a fundamental aspect of human life will be further examined in our later sections in this chapter on feminist theology and process thought. Examining the nature of relationality based squarely on subjectivity in this book presupposes that the human being is a social creature, and that relationships make a difference to the world, indeed they constitute the very fabric of the world's order and chaos. The point to emphasize here is not that relationships and context affect the human being, which they inevitably do, but that the human being affects the world through relationship with it. Decisions leading to actions are taken within this context and this is where our discussion of human agency is focused.

Norms and visions of emancipation and transformation operate in the background here, suggesting that injustice and wrongdoing continue to permeate human reality, and that something ought to be done to transform that. Kant understood Enlightenment as an emancipation from tutelage—from the direction of and obligation to others external to the self. Within the self, obligation to reason and the moral remain powerfully definitive. We can build upon the notion of emancipation in the contemporary world and direct it toward those things which bind human beings and prevent them from deepening their understanding of themselves and their relationships with the world. Human agency allows us a means with which to speak of transforming communities: human beings acting in the world make a difference to the world.

To suggest that human beings can and will shape activity around these norms of emancipation and transformation, means not only that the personal subjectivity of the individual is presupposed, but also that the relational agency of that individual is needed. At the same time, human beings can and will shape activity around norms of destruction and bondage. Freedom brings with it both the possibilities for good and for evil. For purposes of this study, we presuppose the reality of destructive human action in the world, and seek to understand how human beings can participate in bringing about wholeness and well-being out of their relationship with God. This means taking a hopeful and proactive stance with regard to the future of the world. For this reason, the norms of emancipation and transformation guide the conversation.

The human being must be able to make her own decisions about what is needed in any given situation, and for it to have any possibility of making a difference, she must be able to act on this decision. Acting in the world can have consequences ranging from the minute to the global. In each case, the human being makes a specific decision and in this case we shall presume independence and not coercion or fear of punishment. Because of the human being's existence in the world and relationship to the persons and elements in the environment, the action has consequences as well as implications for the future of the world.

Relationality involves transformation, for better or worse. Because the human being is not a solitary self existing in a realm of her own complete control, decisions and actions (subjectivity and agency) change the world. The distinctions between subjectivity and agency, the boundaries of self as mentioned above, must be clearly seen in this, in order to see implications for speaking about human relationships within the world and to the world. This leads us to the contemporary schools of thought which contribute to the conversation about the human being:

> The struggle for women is not to see themselves as a part of a risky relationality, but may be, rather, to affirm their own 'ego boundaries' in psychoanalytic terms, 'intrinsic value' or agency in process terms, or places of plain safety in very practical terms. While understanding all humans as a part of a relational matrix, we can reclaim a positive, healthy understanding of 'separate self' that does not work to undermine relationality, but rather enhances it.[33]

If relationality presumes subjectivity, and is created through agency, then the human being must at some level remain independent, while continually being attended to in terms of relationality. This is the tension seen in the above statement, and one which we will explore in the following sections as we move this to a theological realm, and come to the issue of the human relationship to God.

Contemporary Reflection: Agency, Created Co-Creator, Feminism, and Process Thought

The Challenge of Agency

The impetus for this chapter to speak of agency as a move beyond the boundary of subjectivity mentioned at the outset is a suggestion made by David Kelsey in a discussion of theological anthropology, and its basis in a turn to the subject that is seen as a product of Kant and the Enlightenment. Kelsey's concern is that we be adequately equipped in this contemporary theological era to address human life in its concrete reality, not just in its theoretical and analytical postulation.

> Theological anthropology may be able to deal with persons in their genuine concreteness only by a second 'turn,' from the person as patient or subject of consciousness to the person as agent.[34]

Suggesting a connection to liberation theologies, Kelsey states that, like the move toward the subject we find in the Enlightenment era and the philosophy of Kant explored above, this proposed move toward the agent "promises to be fertile for new constructive proposals of better ways in which to eluci-

---

[33] Marit Trelstad, "Relationality Plus Individuality: The Value of Creative Self Agency," *Dialog* 38 (1999) 198.

[34] Kelsey, "The Human Being," in *Christian Theology*, 192.

date the Christian witness to the liberating and humanizing effect of personal dependence on God."[35] Note the intention here to deal with people in their concreteness, and to seek better ways to express the Christian message of a "liberating and humanizing" relationship with God. These are important reasons for undertaking such a project.

Kelsey's proposal for a turn to the agent is the precise move that this book wishes to take up when speaking about the human being. We need to deal with persons in their genuine concreteness if there is to be any reality of emancipation and liberation within a Christian vision. If it is the world we wish to engage, then we must engage the people located in the world. We must facilitate the relationship between autonomy and relationality in such a way that we can speak of the human being first as autonomous and subject to her own will, now actively engaging in relationship with the world and with God in order to effect transformation and liberation.

What Kelsey alludes to in this challenge is first that developing the idea of human subjectivity is an important step for modern thought. But second, that contemporary theologies inhabit a world in which the "liberating and humanizing effect" of a relationship with God needs to be lifted up and explored. Again, we sense the presupposition of the powers of destruction and bondage that inhabit the world. Moving toward agency allows theologians to examine the way in which human beings can and ought to shape activity in the world. The boundary between subjective thought and conception, and active relating and transforming needs to be crossed. Relationship must presuppose not only individuality, and not just that we are acted upon and formed by our relationships, but particularly the capacity to engage or to act. It is important to note that this conversation about action and human agency has a decidedly philosophical and theological flavor, and does not move to engage the important ethical dimensions of speaking about Christian life.

Moving to the contemporary theological scene, which Kelsey challenges, I will examine some theologians and schools of thought engaging in rethinking the nature of human being. Each of these represents a shift toward thinking of the human being specifically as an agent in some manner and will function throughout this book. I will first examine the particular notion of the human being as created co-creator, and then I will introduce some roots of feminist theology and process thought as schools of thought which pick up on the Kantian vocabulary above in unique and important ways. These schools of thought function as constructive directors for this project.

---

[35] Ibid., 193.

The Created Co-Creator

Philip Hefner's proposal to think of the human being as created co-creator emphasizes agency within the freedom of the human being, who works in cooperation with God for divine purposes. "To be co-creator means that *Homo sapiens* shares self-consciously and responsibly in the formation of the world and its unfolding toward its final consummation under God."[36] The self-consciousness of the human being in her actions, and the responsibility she maintains for the formation of the world, and the movement of it toward God illumine our vocabulary of self-determination and freedom with a decidedly activist bent. Self-consciousness is a philosophical statement that we saw similarly emphasized by Kant. Hefner applies it to human actions here, and insists that it is intrinsic to human nature to be created co-creator with God. Responsibility is the contemporary social and moral component of such decision and action, clarifying the accountability that Kant located in the categorical imperative and morality. The relationship to God forms the overarching, or underlying, theme which becomes more and more apparent in speaking about the human being in this world.

Even more particularly, the proposal of a created co-creator is stated: "Human beings are God's created co-creators whose purpose is to be the *agency, acting* in freedom, to birth the future that is most wholesome for the nature that has birthed us . . . . Exercising this agency is said to be *God's will* for humans"[37] (emphasis mine). The way in which humanity acts to bring about a future in accord with God's will factors into our conversation, and will be explicated in a later chapter. The idea of human agency *as* God's will for humans further provokes our exploration of it as a key component of what it is to be human. If agency is God's will for humans, then it is integral to our very nature; it shapes our lives as a goal, and agency is what drives us and what creates and transforms the world. Human beings without agency, on the contrary, would be mere "patient or subject," as Kelsey stated, moving through life in a less-than-creative manner, so to speak. This presupposes the freedom of subjectivity, and emphasizes the relationship with God that theological anthropology attempts to articulate.

Particular qualification is placed upon the notion of the freedom entailed in this concept of the human being as created co-creator. This is a "freedom in which the human agent must take responsibility for judging whether the conceived action is desirable. Then there is the responsibility for

---

[36] Philip Hefner, "The Human Being," in *Christian Dogmatics*, edited by Carl E. Braaten and Robert W. Jenson (Philadelphia: Fortress, 1984) 326.

[37] Philip Hefner, *The Human Factor: Evolution, Culture, Religion* (Minneapolis: Fortress, 1993) 27.

living with the consequences of the action, even if they prove undesirable."[38] Coupled with the freedom and ability to make and act upon decisions here is the responsibility of living with the consequences, as well as to consent and react to feedback. This fleshes out our Kantian concept of free decision of the human will; we see again how decisions do not exist in vacuums of their own creating. We are not simple solitary subjects rationally and independently going about the business of life. Rather, as we discussed above, actions and decisions have consequences in the worlds we inhabit. This is based partially on the relational nature of the world, and therefore consequences must be dealt with in an appropriate responsive manner. The ideas of responsibility and culpability will be a very important part of the human as created co-creator to which we will return when we move into a brief discussion of the implications for Christology that come with reconstruing anthropology.

In line with the philosophy sketched above, Hefner speaks of freedom within a theory of the created co-creator as it "integrates self-awareness, decision, action, and responsibility . . . ."[39] The concepts of freedom of decision and self-awareness remain, here enhanced with the importance of action and responsibility. Agency is God's will for humans, and we see how the concept of the human being comes to theological fruition here. Integrating subjectivity with agency construes the proposed way of being human and allows us to speak of emancipation and transformation as real possibilities for human beings and the world. To be created is to be in intimate relationship with God, and to be co-creator is to be related, responsible agent in the world.

Introducing Feminist Theology

As Kelsey suggested, contemporary schools of thought, particularly liberation theologies, systematically examine the human being in a way that focuses on and takes seriously their creatureliness; Embodiedness and lived experience become central sources for theology in some contemporary circles. Feminist theology is an example of just such a movement. The current wave of feminist theology gained momentum in the late 1960s and early 1970s with such scholars as Valerie Saiving and Mary Daly, rooted in such previous women writers as Simone deBeauvoir and Virginia Woolf. Saiving's 1960 article entitled "The Human Situation,"[40] placed the question of women's experience at the center of theological controversy. Were women's experiences accounted

---

[38] "The Human Being," 327.

[39] *The Human Factor*, 46.

[40] Valerie Saiving Goldstein, "The Human Situation: a Feminine View," *JR* 40 (1960) 100–12.

for in traditional theological constructions? In Saiving's analysis of Reinhold Neibuhr and Anders Nygren, and

> a widespread tendency in contemporary theology to describe man's predicament as rising from his separateness and the anxiety occasioned by it and to identify sin with self-assertion and love with selflessness,[41]

the answer came out as a resounding "No." Feminist theology grew as a response to this pattern of theological construction which built in part upon the image of Kant's solitary subject. Feminist theologians insisted that the human being cannot be thought of outside of relationships—both for the way in which they have defined the person and the way in which each person defines them. Saiving's particular analysis of a faulty assumption about sin demonstrated one way in which women's experience in the world, one which was decidedly relational, was not taken into account. She illumined the centrality of human experience for any theological conversation, any construction of a concept of God, and any language for God.

Saiving's proposal, modest by current standards, that the dominance of men in the field of theology has resulted in a male-dominated thought-system, opened some doors for women to engage their own experience and reflect on what it means for them to be human. Gender differences began to be a factor in theological reflection, as one's experience in general came to be appreciated for its influence on thought and scholarship. Feminist theologians eventually called for and necessitated space for women to construct theologies from their own experiences as women.

The human situation, as analyzed by "certain contemporary theologians," (Saiving's words) did not account for the feminine view. Having been constructed from the masculine view, theological concepts of the human being were criticized as being limited. The theological positions being criticized by Saiving have direct ties to our image of the human being as solitary subject, as self-contained, rational being. The ideal of what it meant to be human rose out of those notions, and as feminist theologians assert, out of men's experiences as those subjects.

Feminist theology emerged as a way to change the questions. No longer are we to be simply concerned about what it means for a human to be autonomous, self-determined and rational. We must attend to the methods by which we think about and address these questions, and we must take into account the way in which our being human affects what we say about "the human being." A concern for both freedom and relationality becomes

---

[41] Ibid., 100.

particularly coherent when Saiving suggests that the "new way" of rearing daughters is such that they become "independent, differentiated, free human beings of whom some contribution is expected other than the production of the next generation."[42] This statement makes clear the concern for all persons to be able and encouraged in their autonomy and their self-determination. As authentic human beings, she suggests, women have the ability to contribute to society and to reality in a way that is not solely determined by their biological capabilities. The tension between individuality and relationality remains, but as something to be lifted up, not resolved.

The unique approach of feminist theology as it emerges is that it criticizes traditional Christian theology for failing to account for women in generalized presentations of "the human being." Feminist theologians insist that women's experiences have often been the very opposite of such "ideal" human nature. Freedom, when implemented by women, comes to mean more than independence. As women began to take seriously the examination of what it is to be human, they began to reveal their experiences within a less-than-free realm of male-dominated institutions and social realms. Further, the very ideals of humanity come under intense criticism beginning with Saiving, as she challenges the notion of sin as self-assertion, when in fact that is often the very trait denied to and missing from "a feminine view."

Mary Daly, in her first book, *The Church and the Second Sex*,[43] likewise critically examines the patterns of male-dominated religion and the institutional church, and asks a question dating back to French theorist Simone deBeauvoir's work: Are women doomed to be eternally Other, the second sex? Like Saiving, Daly critically engages what it means to be human, as she examines Christian tradition and its failures to account for women's experience and sense of what it means to be human. She puts the question before the eyes of the church, examining historical doctrine and practices regarding the exclusion of women and their experiences. As a work coming directly out of the era of Vatican II, and as a response to her own attendance at this event, this text concerns itself specifically with the history of Catholic doctrine as well as contemporary papal documents. Daly argued that the Christian tradition stereotyped women and limited their roles not only in society, but especially in the church.

She says, "Catholic teaching has prolonged a traditional view of woman which at the same time idealizes and humiliates her."[44] The inferiority of

---

[42] Ibid., 110.

[43] Mary Daly, *The Church and the Second Sex: With the Feminist Postchristian Introduction and New Archaic Afterwords by the Author* (Boston: Beacon, 1985).

[44] Ibid., 53.

women is proposed by the church to be biblically based and divinely ordained. Daly counters this, and calls for women to engage in these conversations about what it means to be human, to respond "to that liberating Power which calls us to transcend the archaic heritage and move toward a future whose seeds are already within us."[45] This signifies God's activity in our human be-ing. Daly insists that we ought to take those abilities that we already have within us and create a future accordingly. Human agency and independence are grounded in God, and directed toward a future of liberation. She speaks here of God as a transcendent dimension of our experience, ever compelling forward motion toward a freedom that in its fullest sense includes the consciousness of all human beings. Hefner's language of birthing reality in accordance with God's will puts forth a similar sense.

Daly's work takes a major philosophical shift as she later moves to a radical reclamation of women's experience as sole norm in constructing reality. What remains is the deep concern for understanding what it means to be human in the world, and for her, the question is more specifically what does it mean to be woman in a patriarchal world. She assigns responsibility for misogyny to patriarchy, and constructs a world in which women are woman-identified, the true connection to biophilic forces likened to that which she abandons, God.[46] Our philosophical vocabulary words like autonomy and self-determination take on a creative new spin within Daly's system of thought. Here, the autonomy of women is their liberation from patriarchally controlled environments, both psychic and physical. To be self-determined is to be free from the control of male-dominated institutions and doctrines.

Again, we are reminded of Kant's disparaging account of the human being under tutelage, under the guidance or direction of and obligation to another, and his call *Sapere aude!* Know boldly! Enlightenment takes on a fresh face when considered in the context of Daly's feminist philosophy. For her, to be human is to be woman-identified in a physical world which seeks the destruction of life. Knowing boldly is seeing the forces of destruction and having the courage to name them, dis-cover the forces of life and celebrate with them. To be woman-identified is to be in touch with the deep biophilic powers of life, and to be in opposition to the necrophilic state of patriarchy. Liberation is first and ultimately psychic, and a woman's independence is marked by her relationships with other women and "elemental creatures."[47]

---

[45] Ibid., 222.

[46] These shifts are seen in Daly's *Beyond God the Father: Toward a Philosophy of Women's Liberation* (Boston: Beacon, 1973), and *Pure Lust: Elemental Feminist Philosophy* (Boston: Beacon, 1984).

[47] "Elemental *adj* ["characterized by stark simplicity, naturalness, or unrestrained or undisciplined vigor or force . . . CRUDE, PRIMITIVE, FUNDAMENTAL, BASIC, EARTHY"

Naming is the base for construction of reality, can even be seen as a manifestation of co-creating, and Daly traces it back to the story of Adam as the first human being, and his ability and responsibility to name the things around him in the world. Citing Paulo Freire, she says:

> To exist humanly is to name the self, the world, and God. The 'method' of the evolving spiritual consciousness of women is nothing less than this beginning to speak humanly—a reclaiming of the right to name. The liberation of language is rooted in the liberation of ourselves.[48]

Naming empowers the formation and the transformation of the world surrounding the individual human being. Naming is grounded in human agency, and is a form of actively engaging the world.

These brief introductions to two feminist theologians demonstrate a definitive concern for the human condition, particularly as embodied by women. What feminist theology offers that diverges from other modern modes of thought is an emphasis on the experience of female human beings and the necessity of speaking of women in particular as agents of their own reality. It takes freedom and the importance of self-determination seriously. It presumes the way in which context and situation determine the human being, and asks how the human being can determine her own context and situation. It assesses the role of this situation and context in terms of theological and philosophical construction. It is based on the distinctive character of women's experience within the world, generally criticized as male-dominated. Because of this position, it is generally concerned with liberation from patriarchal modes of thought and life. In accord with the emphasis on freedom and self-determination, it becomes theologically important to emphasize the ability of women to name reality, to name their experience of God, and to name God.

Kant's categorical imperative can be integrated into feminist thought, as Saiving and Daly point out the ways in which patriarchy and the Christian tradition have utilized the female person and the feminine principle, effectively treating "woman" as a means. If we were to work under the guise of Kant's philosophical notion that each person be treated not as a thing to be used as a means to some other end, but as an end in herself, we would be compelled to insist upon women's ability to name reality, to participate in creating the future, and to rationally decide her own fates. Political movements identified with women's liberation can find particular resonance with this notion, in terms of social justice and activism.

—Webster's]" in Mary Daly with Jane Caputi, *Websters' First New Intergalactic Wickedary of the English Language* (Boston: Beacon, 1987) 72.

[48] *Beyond God the Father*, 8.

Introducing Process Thought

Participation in and active shaping of reality is integral to process theology in ways similar to and distinct from feminist theology. The foundation for the philosophy and theology called "process," is experience, broadly and specifically understood. Based upon the metaphysical system of Alfred North Whitehead, process theologians take as central to any construction the definitive nature of experience for reality.

> He gave particular priority to the data of religious experience. Therefore, even though his model of reality reflects his highly technical background, it ultimately rests upon a broad understanding of experience in a relativity-conscious age. By using this model to express Christian faith, we push toward the rewards of communicating Christian faith in thought forms that reflect a contemporary understanding of reality.[49]

As in feminist theological scholarship, reflecting a contemporary view of reality is central to process thought. As theologians engaging a feminist approach seek to reflect a contemporary view of reality that includes all human experience, theologians engaging the process model take seriously modern scientific accounts of reality. Both seek to account for the world as it "really" is.

In the process model, experience is the basis for the entire composition of the world, from molecules to aggregate objects like rocks, to plant life and human life. Experience is itself a process, and thus is an inescapable part of reality. As such, a contemporary theology built upon this philosophical foundation can emphasize the definitive power of human experience, the power of the human being herself, and the power of the world in relationship with God. Each occasion and entity in the world continually experiences the objective past, the potential of its future, and the process through which it moves in order to actualize. The continual nature of this is the process; process entails continual creation and perpetual perishing (Whitehead's phrase) throughout the life of an entity or occasion.

Power, in the process model, is a relational and mutual force that is shared by God and the world. It is self-determination writ large: "The essence of power is the drive towards aesthetic worth for its own sake.... It constitutes the drive of the universe.... It is final cause, maintaining in the creature its appetite for creation."[50] Human beings possess a capability to choose, a responsibility for those choices, and an obligation to respond to the consequences; again, this is seen as characteristic of the process that is reality.

---

[49] Marjorie Hewitt Suchocki, *God–Christ–Church: A Practical Guide to Process Theology* (New York: Crossroad: 1982, 1989) 4.

[50] Alfred North Whitehead, *Modes of Thought* (New York: Macmillan, 1966) 119.

The drive toward worth, spoken of in theological terms, is undergirded by and guided toward God. God exists in this model as a lure, as a source of potentiality. Whitehead's technical understanding states that God provides the initial aim for each actual entity in the world, providing it with the best possible option for actualization. But divine power does not control the entity's actual decision (actualization), rather lures it toward God, with what we may understand as hope for the best possible decision. God and the world find in each other the mutuality required for enhanced existence. Neither controls the other, but each needs that which is provided by the other. The affinities with the model of a created co-creator lie in the way God and the world are working together to bring about the world.

The terminology we drew out of Kant's writing comes up briefly in Whitehead's thought. Reflecting his technical use of terms, we read: "[T]he subjective aim limits the ontological principle by its own autonomy."[51] The ontological principle is defined as "no actual entity, no reason."[52] Stated another way, Whitehead understands that this principle is "the first step in the description of the universe as a solidarity of many actual entities."[53] Autonomy, here, is that which defines the character of the human being, setting its limits, or its boundaries as we have spoken of earlier. Autonomy is a limit principle on the ontological principle. It is an independence which is conditioned by general particularities, i.e., species, category of existence, location, and relations. This is the solidarity of many actual entities.

Further, "self-determination is always imaginative in its origin."[54] To be determined by the self, autonomously establishing limits on existence, requires imagination. This is not imagination as in allowing one to believe in unicorns (or maybe so!) but imagination understood alongside difference and novelty. Imaginative origins suggest that the self determines its future in terms of a creative, novel integration of past and possible. Reason fits in with this in a somewhat different way: "The function of Reason is to promote the art of life . . . . Fatigue is the antithesis of Reason."[55] The art of life could be interpreted as the energies to actualize novelty, to bring about a future in the spirit of imaginative generation, self-generating, of course. As a proposed antithesis to reason, fatigue embodies a lack of motivators, absence of action, and perhaps even inability to actualize. Actualization is an inescapable fact

---

[51] Whitehead, *Process and Reality: An Essay in Cosmology* (New York: Macmillan, 1976) 244.
[52] Ibid., 19.
[53] Ibid., 40.
[54] Ibid., 245.
[55] Whitehead, *The Function of Reason* (Boston: Beacon, 1929, 1958) 4, 23.

of existence—to exist is to be in the process of actualization, ever becoming more of what one is.

Freedom likewise fits into the metaphysical scheme that undergirds Whitehead's thought. "The freedom inherent in the universe is constituted by this element of self-causation."[56] Self-causation, or self-determination as spoken of above, characterizes freedom in the universe, and Whitehead does not limit this to the scope of human freedom, rather it is a metaphysical self-causation in which all actual entities participate. Within the realm of possibility and past reality, each actual entity makes real its own particular existence, freely.

The extent to which an actuality is capable of exercising imagination and introducing novelty determines the degree of its freedom. The plant in my living room is limited by the size of its pot, the soil I have potted it in, and the whim of my watering habits. It still struggles to grow, to actualize longer vines and fuller leaves, to the extent which it is capable. My cats are limited by the size of my home, their food and water supply, and the fact that we decided to have their front claws removed. They struggle to keep themselves entertained with various household objects, and to care for themselves and each other. I am limited by my social location, my physical body, my history of decisions. I struggle to deepen relationships with family and friends, and discern greater meaning and purpose for a human life in relationship to God, to the extent that I am able. Each of us is in the process of becoming, actualizing, growing into something more of who we are.

As a final point, we must note how important relationality is to process thought, and the way in which Whitehead addresses "the problem of the solidarity of the universe."

> The answer given by the organic philosophy is the doctrine of prehensions, involved in concrescent integrations, and terminating in a definite, complex unity of feeling. To be actual must mean that all actual things are alike objects, enjoying objective immortality in fashioning creative actions; and that all actual things are subjects, each prehending the universe from which it arises.[57]

Integration, prehension, and feeling are all ways to say that each entity in the world takes in the existence of others, and that each entity in the world acts in the particular context in which it exists. The presumed subjectivity of all entities establishes the independence and ability to perceive and discern the reality of the world around them. The principle of relativity which Whitehead employs insists that each entity in the world participates in the concrescence

---

[56] *Process and Reality*, 88.
[57] Ibid., 56.

of the other—presenting the inescapable webbed nature of reality. With these concepts of relationality and actuality, Whitehead's philosophy provides a rich basis for theological construction, as we will see in the following chapter.

Moving Forward to Contemporary Constructive Options

Along with the notion of a created co-creator, process thought and feminist theology, as they have been introduced here, play off of some of the key concepts of an Enlightenment turn to the subject. They introduce an element of novelty, however, in the insistence upon speaking of the human being more thoroughly as relational agent, as able to effect transformation in the world, as capable and responsible. They do this in that over and above speaking of the human being as autonomous, as self-determined and free to decide, as subject of her own will, as Kant effectively did, they now emphasize and develop the way in which the human being is able to act out of that subjectivity, perhaps with some intentionality for transforming the world.

This crosses the fine boundary between subject and agent. The solitary subject is the figure of Kant's Enlightenment era moral thinker; the relational agent is the contemporary socially conscious and active individual. This book intends to build upon the resources that we find in Kantian philosophy, taking into account the concerns for the contemporary world found in feminist theology and process thought. The concerns fundamentally center on what it means to be human, and they move out from there to understanding the human being's relationship to the world and to God, as well as nuancing the relationship between God and the world. This is how I understand theological anthropology for this project.

The concern for an anthropological dimension of theology predates the Enlightenment, and is in fact a fundamental characteristic of Christian theology. "The foundation for a theological concentration on the human person was already laid in the early Christian faith in the incarnation of God."[58] Pannenberg appropriately makes the point that while modern theological anthropology is informed by and indeed shaped in part by the Enlightenment, it taps into deep matters of faith and of the character of the religion. The foundation which is the incarnation makes the very notion of what it is to be human a very important consideration for any theology within the Christian realm. Human being itself becomes a vehicle for revelation and relation between God and the human being. For this precise reason, it makes sense to address the problems of atonement and Christology previously introduced, through a study of the relationship between God and the human being.

---

[58] Pannenberg, *Anthropology in Theological Perspective*, 12.

Theological anthropology understood this way equips us to propose solutions to certain dilemmas of atonement, and allow us to make proposals for an understanding of sacramental theology. The philosophical terms help us to situate the conversation in the modern realm, and the theological implications drive us deeper into the issues.

Further, Pannenberg cites some dangers in acknowledging the anthropological dimension of theology. "It is the danger that human beings doing theology may be concerned only with themselves instead of with God and thus let the true subject matter of theology go by the board."[59] It is for this reason that this project holds in direct tension and relation both the question of what it means for one to be human, and what it means for God to be God. It is in the location of their meeting that each is seen in its full viability. What makes God worthy of worship? What makes humans worthy of God? A fundamental concern, therefore, lies in the relationship. This is what will lead us, in chapter three, to examine that moment in Christian theology wherein the relationship between God and the human being is made manifest: the sacraments. This will be done through a thinker who is thoroughly theo-centered: Martin Luther.

To return to Kelsey's challenges: He poses some questions which compel us to further examine contemporary theologies.

> Is not the concept 'subject' in modern theology fatally flawed for the purposes of Christian theology precisely because it reflects a Western, male, bourgeois status that has the requisite surplus of time beyond what is needed to sustain life, but only as the fruit of other people's oppression?[60]

The solitary subject as we have come to know it here is suggestively inadequate for speaking of the human condition today, precisely because of such efforts as those in feminist theologies, process thought, and other anthropologically minded theologians. These theologies, as manifestations of a liberation-minded contemporary era, have constructive offerings to make which can make a significant difference for the Christian tradition, particularly as it has been critically addressed in feminist theology. We must speak about the human being in such a way that he/she is fully understood to be an agent, an independent, social being able to effect emancipation and transformation in the world.

We find in Kelsey one final provocative question: "Have theologians evaded the hard question about reconciling finite human autonomy with

---

[59] Ibid., 16.
[60] Kelsey, "The Human Being," 191.

radical dependency on God?"[61] Have we tended to fall on the side of either preserving the utter privacy of our thoughts, or living wholly as patient and subject of God's will? The gray area of relationality in the God-human dynamic needs to be illumined here, and will build upon the discussion of freedom and relationality we have seen arising from philosophical terms. We can no longer leave it all up to God, nor can we assume that we are able to do and be everything. What does it mean to be both autonomous and dependent? Is that even possible? We can find this question applicable to human relationships, as well as to the human relationship with God. What does it mean to take seriously both the relationship that we as human beings have with God, and the responsibility that we have as actors in this world? To be both created and co-creator? "But surely the hard questions come when one considers persons not as patients but as finite agents—active concrete powers in a shared and public world—and when one tries to reconcile the autonomy of finite agency with dependency on God."[62]

Agency occurs within the "shared and public world," and therefore necessitates relationality. Relationships must be attended to and dealt with as they affect and construct human life. The first step in theological anthropology is tied to the philosophical affirmation that human beings are autonomous, rational, self-determined creatures with moral capabilities. The next step is to say that human beings have not only moral capability of decision, but social capability to effect change. The challenge is to understand the relationship between God and the human being in this context of concrete manifestation. This insists that we deal with human being in the world, and that we make some way of understanding God's relationship to that. "For this agency to enjoy its fullest sense of being, it must have the freedom and creativity to respond uniquely to the influences given to it."[63]

Recognizing that injustice continues to pervade modern societies, we must claim that human beings have a *responsibility* based on a *capability* to effect real transformation in this world. Capability assumes a metaphysical fact, responsibility assumes a moral dimension. We must not always depend on the goodness of God to rectify all things. We must claim the ability and the culpability that goes along with the agency of being human, especially if that is God's will for us. Further exploration of particular theologians' constructions offered in the realms of feminist and process thought develop this claim, and deepen our understanding of the relationship between God and the human being.

---

[61] Ibid.
[62] Ibid.
[63] Trelstad, "Relationality Plus Individuality," 197.

2

Human Agency and Divine Mutuality:

Feminist Theologies and Process Thought

In the course of this chapter, I will present a few detailed proposals for understanding humanity with specific attention toward agency, and for speaking about God in relationship to that humanity. The concepts examined in this chapter work with feminist and process principles as introduced in the preceding chapter. As we build on the philosophical basis that has been introduced, this chapter will show how particular theologians construct an understanding of the human being, of God, and of the relationship between God and the human being that addresses our shift from subjectivity to agency. The theological implications of this shift have been raised by David Kelsey's challenge, and we seek here to further understand the nuanced relationship between the human being and God in some constructive proposals offered by contemporary theologians.

This chapter will play a large part in our later assessment of Christology and atonement in light of the relationship between God and the human being. A conception of the relationship between God and the world precedes an understanding of the role of Jesus as God incarnate, and interpretations of atonement within Christian tradition. Ultimately, what we say about the relationship between God and the human being is concretely manifest not only in the stories of Jesus as Christ, but also in the sacraments of Christianity. The webbed nature of theology leads us to examine all of these areas: What we say about the relationship between God and the human being affects how we understand the events of Jesus' life and death, and likewise, the way in which we understand those events impacts our theology of the sacraments, particularly the eucharist.

The theological proposals of this chapter will function in relationship with traditional resources examined in the following chapter. This chapter locates the critical component of the book in the contemporary scene and will allow us to assess effectively the importance and impact of Luther's theological writings on the sacraments of the Christian church for theological anthropology as we understand it here. Luther will likewise serve as a challenge to and a critic of these contemporary theological approaches. We will see what is being said about God, about the human being, and about their relationship by select feminist and process theologians, and we will see how these theologies build upon the philosophical resources for speaking about humanity identified in the first chapter. In the scope of the book, we will seek to understand how these proposals resonate aspects of traditional Christian resources, how these theologians may be criticized by a traditional approach such as Luther's, and in what ways they offer criticism and/or a more appropriate contemporary response.

At this moment of the journey, we must see in detail how the relationship between God and the human being can be and is being construed. I have chosen contemporary, liberation-minded theologians who take with blatant seriousness the role of experience and so-called "worldly" affairs in theological construction. The proposals which are entertained in this chapter provide insight into the human being and her relationship with God. I believe that honesty about one's location in and relationship to experience is characteristic of much contemporary theological conversation. It is also a guiding principle of this project to take seriously the call for emancipation and transformation within the world as we inhabit it. Both the feminist attention to social justice and the process attention to the metaphysical givens ground the theologies that spin out from the core principles. Each operates with an eye toward the transformative power of the world, both physical and psychic.

We will begin by exploring some theological proposals presented by four women theologians and their attempts to address what it means to be human, what it means for God to be God, and what it means that God and the human being are in relationship. I have titled the section "feminist" theological anthropology, although not all of the women name themselves as "feminist." All of them do share in some aspect of feminist theology, namely the attention to sexism within Christian tradition and secular communities, but two locate themselves simultaneously within communities concerned with liberation that goes beyond gender. Quoting Anna Julia Cooper, one theologian insists: The world needs to hear all of women's voices across color lines. I will then briefly address the relationship between feminist and process theologies, and move on to present some theological implications from process principles. This will involve not only Whitehead's work, but also the work of three select process theologians who speak to the concerns of this project.

"Feminist" Theological Anthropology: Select Readings

Agency and Responsibility

One particularly helpful contribution to feminist theological anthropology is Beverly Harrison's feminist construction of moral agency. In "The Power of Anger in the Work of Love," Harrison combines what she calls naturalistic metaphors for God with an emphasis upon the practical and radical creativity, activity, and responsibility of human beings.[1] Within the concept of practical creativity, she insists that there be a fundamental connection maintained between do-ing and be-ing. "In my opinion, the metaphor of Be-ing does not permit us to incorporate the radicality of human agency adequately. *Doing* must be as fundamental as be-ing in our theologies."[2] In constructing a feminist moral theology, Harrison emphasizes the active and creative aspect of being human in the world. It is not enough to speak of be-ing, to develop an appropriate ontology. It is not sufficient to ask what it is to "be" human, but we must face what it means to "do" as a human. Any sense of being must be connected to human doing. The two must function together in a feminist theology, developing a fuller sense of what it means to be a human "being," "doing" in this world. This is practical creativity. This informs our present understanding of human agency not spoken of in the technical philosophical sense, but in the general, theological framework. Harrison's concept of human agency suggests that humans engage in the work of love.

This doing, or human action, she says, is particularly spoken of as acts of love. Humans have the power both to "act-each-other-into-well-being " (love) as well as "to thwart life and to maim each other. The fateful choice is ours . . . ."[3] Responsibility is a key element of this construction. We have both the power and the choice to enact well-being or bring harm to the world. Also key is the presence of God as the power of love in the world, which is embraced by and acted upon by human beings. The decisive moment is if we choose to "set free the power of God's love in the world . . . ."[4] This makes it the *work* of love. Responsibility accompanies the choices that humans have

---

[1] Beverly Harrison, "The Power of Anger in the Work of Love," in *Making the Connections: Essays in Feminist Social Ethics,* ed. Carol S. Robb (Boston: Beacon, 1985) 10; orig. pub. 1980.

[2] Ibid., 10.

[3] Ibid., 11.

[4] Ibid.

before them, to act for life and love or to distort the same reality. The power of God lies in the presence of love, what we will later call the lure toward a vision of order. Harrison ties human moral agency to the life of Jesus, and we will develop that in the fourth chapter of this book.

In the context of her proposal, Harrison speaks of the power of anger as an element of practical human activity.

> Anger is not the opposite of love. It is better understood as a feeling-signal that all is not well in our relation to other persons or groups or to the world around us. Anger is a mode of connectedness to others and it is always a vivid form of caring . . . . Such anger is a signal that change is called for, that transformation in relations is required.[5]

As a human emotion, reaction, or sense, anger serves us in that it warns of a wrongness in relation. It signifies that we care about what is happening, and it is a form of connection that involves us deeply in the world. When we care enough to be angry, that is a sign that there is need for transformation. It is somewhat similar to a discussion of pain, and the question, is pain ever a good thing? Yes, pain often is a signifier that something is wrong in our bodies. Pain tells us when to stop, when to seek help, when our physical limits have been reached.

Likewise, anger tells us when our relations are stretched, distorted, or just plain wrong. Anger compels us to action. We have colorful expressions for such states of being: "I was so mad that I could have spit nails." Anger tells us when our emotional or spiritual limits have been broached. Consider this scenario: I was walking down the street in my neighborhood, a busy street, on my way to an appointment, in the middle of the afternoon. A banged up car with two men in it pulled up beside me, following me, driving very slowly. The men proceeded to make lurid, sexist, and crude comments to me. When it was clear that they were not moving on, I cussed at them, and hollered at them to get the hell away from me. They laughed and sped off. I was so taken aback by this blatant crass behavior in the middle of a sunny afternoon on a busy street that I was simultaneously afraid and angry. I made sure that I had my keychain safety whistle at the ready, looked around to be sure that there were others within shouting distance, and prepared myself should they choose to come back on foot. I fumed all the rest of the day and week that I was made to feel so defensive. In the middle of the afternoon! On a busy street! Near a world-renowned hospital and academic institution!

Anger, pain, and fear function in our lives as animal-like signifiers of distortion, whether it be in physical health and safety, emotional readiness, or relationships within the social world. My fear at the incident on the street

---

[5] Ibid., 14.

compelled me to ready myself for an impending attack. My anger signified that there is something wrong in a world where this is commonplace behavior. It was not merely my anger at the two men in the car, but an anger at the distorted social situations which breed that kind of activity, which makes me feel unsafe when walking down a busy street near my home on a sunny afternoon. It is an anger that compels me to seek transformation in the world, signifying that I care about relations within the world.

Relationality, for Harrison, is the essential nature of the world, "the heart of all things."[6] Our involvement in the web of life not only has theological implications but it has a decidedly ethical dimension. We are called to be partners with each other and with God in a manner that reflects a deeply mutual love, "love that has both the quality of a gift received and the quality of a gift given."[7] Criticizing traditional autonomous and detached notions of divinity, feminist moral theology as Harrison proposes bases itself squarely in relationality. This is a relationality of full, mutual participating beings, acting each other into well-being.

We will return to Harrison's proposal and her attempt to address the implications of this concept of human moral agency for understanding the life and death of Jesus. For now, we emphasize the work of love and the power of anger to compel human action in accord with the vision of God. To set free the love of God in the world requires tremendous human commitment and strength, to be found in relationships.

What does it mean to be human in Harrison's construction? To be human is to act in the world; To be human is to bear responsibility for one's actions in the world; To be human is to be in relationship. These things are elements of our working definition of human agency, and we see some ways in which they affect theological construction. Harrison expresses her own commitment to justice and liberation in the way in which she presents the human being as situated and actively participating in the creation of reality. This is for better or for worse, although the hope is that humanity works for the better, for the love of God.

What does it mean for God to be God in Harrison's vision? God is love, God is presence and power and the foundation of human relationship. God is also radical: "It is risky to live as if the commonwealth of the living God were present—that is, to live by radical mutuality and reciprocity."[8] As the basis for radical mutuality and reciprocity, God present in the world challenges human distortion and denial. The fact that humanity has a "fateful choice"

---

[6] Ibid., 15.

[7] Ibid., 18.

[8] Ibid., 19.

means that the choice for the worse will sometimes be made, and in those situations, God's presence in the world is a threat, a counter-reality.

The relationship between God and the human being for Harrison has the potential to be a radically life-affirming and creative union. For the human being to act in accord with the vision of God for a commonwealth of radical mutuality and reciprocity means that God's power can be fully unleashed into the world. God's power of love has the capacity to transform the world beyond itself, but only through the activity of humanity. For Harrison, the incarnation is central to this vision, and we will see how her proposal expands on this in a later chapter.

Relationality and Freedom

Further contribution toward theological reconstruction is seen in the origins of a *mujerista* anthropology offered by Ada María Isasi-Díaz. By word of criticism of the very kind of anthropology which we saw developed in the philosophical basis of the first chapter, Isasi-Díaz says: "Modern theology's anthropology revolves around a so-called bourgeois subject characterized by a freedom based on rationalism and individualism." And she further contrasts this with

> the anthropology of Latin American liberation theology [which] centers on the poor, on those who suffer, on those who have been ignored by history and are not only marginal but considered and treated by the power elites as superfluous population.[9]

The experience of Hispanic women in the world offers a different starting point for talking about what it means to be human in the world, and to be in relationship with God. No longer can the image of the bourgeois, individual, rational subject be considered sufficient for speaking about the human condition. The stark difference between these two central figures demonstrates the difference between a traditional approach to anthropology and a *mujerista* theology.

Isasi-Díaz formulates *mujerista* anthropology with the presupposition that theology "was lacking a key element that has since become the core of our work: providing a platform for the voices of Hispanic Women."[10] Using the voices and lived experience of Latinas as primary source, her theological construction works toward liberation within the Hispanic communities, the academic realm, and the larger Christian communities. She primarily seeks a

---

[9] Ada María Isasi-Díaz, *En La Lucha, In the Struggle: Elaborating a Mujerista Theology—A Hispanic Women's Liberation Theology* (Minneapolis: Fortress, 1993) 168.
[10] Ibid., 1.

way in which to understand the moral agency of Hispanic women, to name the protagonism that has been ignored or denied throughout history. Because of the struggle with sexism, *mujerista* theology as she proposes it here shares both a critical and a constructive character with feminist theology as we have seen in Harrison, Valerie Saiving, and Mary Daly.

The unique character of this proposal is its location in Hispanic communities. Isasi-Díaz uses three particular elements that she draws from her location in the proposal to explicate the specificity of Hispanic women's experience: *la lucha, permítanme hablar,* and *la familia/la comunidad*. Each represents something essential about what it is to be a woman within the Hispanic community. Each offers up a resource for theology, and touches on areas of moral agency that are of particular concern to this project's attempt to deepen that concept. Isasi-Díaz's reflection on a *mujerista* anthropology under these three distinctions provides us a creative manner in which to speak of human agency.

La lucha is "the struggle" which is part of daily life for women. "Of course the centrality of struggle as a constitutive element of the everyday lives of Latinas, of Latinas' self-construction, can be understood and grasped only against a background of oppression due to specific historical injustices . . . ."[11] This concept does not in any way encourage suffering, but acknowledges its role in life. As a part of experience, it is a part of what informs theology, because it informs what it means to be human. Struggle is seen both in the daily toils of human life and in the historical reality in which women find themselves. Indeed the daily struggle to be woman is couched in a long history of patriarchal social and theological structures.

Isasi-Díaz suggests that Hispanic women have the "ability to deal with suffering, without being determined by it."[12] The emphasis placed on struggle, and not on suffering, enables the focus to remain on the agency of women to effectively deal with daily experiences in the world. She particularly notes her divergence from other Latin American liberation theologians in not locating Latinas primarily in suffering, but in the struggle. "To consider suffering as what locates us would mean that we understand ourselves not as a moral subject but as one acted upon by the oppressors."[13] A refusal to be determined by suffering assumes the ability to transform or to work out of whatever experiences of suffering may come upon the individual or the community. Rather than emphasize the experience of being acted upon, Isasi-Díaz emphasizes

---

[11] Ibid.,168.

[12] Ada María Isasi-Díaz, "Elements of a Mujerista Anthropology," in *In the Embrace of God: Feminist Approaches to Theological Anthropology,* ed. Ann O'Hara Graff (Maryknoll, N.Y.: Orbis, 1995) 90.

[13] *En La Lucha*, 168.

the experience of struggling against and within the world.[14] "If what locates Latinas is *la lucha*, then we will be seen not only as a strategic force in history but rather as historical, moral subjects, aware of our own role in defining and bringing about a preferred future."[15] The struggle is the time and place in which human agency is most demanded and most valued. It presents both the challenge to and the opportunity for action.

Isasi-Díaz's second phrase that defines her *mujerista* anthropology, *permítanme hablar*, "allow me to speak," touches once again on the power of language raised in the discussion of naming as agency from Daly. "Because a name ... provides the conceptual framework, the point of reference, the mental constructs that are used in thinking, understanding, and relating . . . ."[16] Indeed she discusses the importance of phrases to name a group of people, such as "Hispanic Women," "Latinas," "*feministas hispanas*," and so on in the language of her own text. She opts to vacillate between the first two phrases, noting the tendency for the dominant U.S. culture to put groups under one name, "more easily to control and assimilate us."[17] A moral agent must have the ability and the freedom to speak, to name reality, to name herself, and to define her relationships to the world around her. In accord with locating Hispanic women's experience *en la lucha*, this phrase is used to emphasize the necessity for and the power of speaking from that location.

When Latinas use the phrase, *permítanme hablar*, she points out that they are "asking for a respectful silence from all those who have the power to set up definitions of what it is to be human,"[18] not asking for permission to speak. In this phrase, the request implies a demand for respect. Let me tell *you* how it is. A focus on women's experience involves telling women's stories, describing their past involvement in creating history, describing the continued power that women have to shape reality, and describing the feelings that go along with their experience of history. "Our insistence on speaking is not only a matter of making known our past; it is also a matter of participating in making present and future history, of being protagonists, of being *agents*

---

[14] Audre Lorde's distinctive definitions of pain and suffering come to mind here. She understands pain as "an event, an experience that must be recognized, named, and then used in some way ... to be transformed. ... Suffering, on the other hand, is the nightmare reliving of unscrutinized and unmetabolized pain." To speak of pain rather than suffering is to embrace the human ability to deal with difficulty and to move on from traumatic experience. *Sister Outsider: Essays and Speeches* (Freedom, Calif.: Crossing, 1996) 171.

[15] *En La Lucha*, 169.

[16] Ibid., 2.

[17] Ibid., 3.

[18] "Elements of a Mujerista Anthropology," 95.

of our own history."[19] Speaking transforms the world and our perceptions of social order. This is what it means to be an agent of one's own history.

As agents of their history and future, Hispanic women struggle for liberation for themselves and for their community. Isasi-Díaz makes this clear and insists that the struggle begins with denouncing the roots of oppression. "Denunciation as part of Latinas' *proyecto histórico* is a challenge to understand and deal with present reality in the name of the future."[20] Coupled with this speaking against oppressive structures that bring destruction and dehumanization to Latinas in particular, we find that annunciation and creation of alternate reality offer a constructive option for the world. "[A]nnunciation becomes reality in our struggle to find or create spaces for self-determination, a key factor in the struggle for liberation."[21] Again, the struggle is the location and the speaking is the agency. *Permítanme hablar*, I have something to say: something to speak against and something to speak into being.

Finally, in her third key phrase, Isasi-Díaz lifts up the role of *la familia/la comunidad*, "the family/the community," as essential to the formation of a *mujerista* anthropology. "[I]n many ways, family has been Latinas' domain through the ages. It is in *la familia* that we are agents of our own history."[22] It is important to take this resource, this power base, and expand protagonism throughout *la comunidad*, for and among all people. Despite the exploitation and objectification of Latina women that often has occurred in the context of family, this concept remains "a grounding factor," one which demonstrates the connection between individual and community, the meeting place between the two found in the Latina woman. It also provides a basis for expanding power that already exists, and opportunity to expose the history of injustice within that very context.

A particular concept of community, *comunidad de fe*, "community of faith," intertwines the power of community and the relationship with the divine. "It is not only a matter of believing that God is with us in our daily struggle, but that we can and do relate to God the same way we relate to all our loved ones."[23] The relationship to God is exemplary of how we do and how we ought to relate to each other within the community, particularly the *comunidad de fe*. Likewise, Isasi-Díaz recognizes that sin is the violation of relationship within the community and it hurts the relationship with the divine. As sin has structural implications, she encourages that communities

---

[19] Ibid., 93, my emphasis.
[20] *En La Lucha*, 36.
[21] Ibid.
[22] "Elements of a Mujerista Anthropology," 97.
[23] *En La Lucha*, 39.

need to be praxis-oriented, bringing together "personal support and community action . . . ."[24] There is a flow between the human being and God, and the human being and the community in this concept, one that builds upon and establishes relationships of trust and commitment.

Within Isasi-Díaz's proposal for a *mujerista* anthropology, the human being is located in struggle. This location simultaneously demands and challenges the agency of the person to name her reality, her history and her future within the community. Shifting from a liberation emphasis on suffering as it defines human experience to the struggle as it characterizes daily life, this proposal calls forth human moral agency, individual protagonism within a community of faith and relationships with the world and the divine.

A concept of God underlies this proposal as one who is continually revealed "in the midst of and through the community of faith . . . ."[25] That God is manifest in daily life is a given, and it is a source of strength for the struggle. The relationship between God and the human being is imaged as that of partners in the struggle, God in the midst of the struggle, *en la lucha*. God's presence to and with the human being undergirds the sense of hope and protagonism that Isasi-Díaz's mujerista anthropology presents. This sense of hope and protagonism is coupled, however, with a palpable sense of reality and struggle as inescapable characteristics of human life, particularly the human lives of Hispanic women. Working toward and with God, however, remains a fundamental part of this proposal.

Creativity and Capability

Womanist theology provides rich resources for understanding what it means to be human as a woman within a liberation-minded African-American community. Within the context of a dialogical systematic theology written with her husband Garth, Karen Baker-Fletcher sketches out seven metaphors, or symbolizations of "Black women's participation in God's creative activity . . ."[26] that will be detailed below. It is critical for Baker-Fletcher to see black women's activity as particular participation in God's creation, as a way to reclaim the value of experience which has been long devalued and ignored. The definition of "womanist" for theology draws from Alice Walker's words, which include: "Traditionally capable, as in: 'Mama, I'm walking to Canada and I'm taking you and a bunch of other slaves with me.'"[27] Capability is a

---

[24] Ibid., 40.

[25] Ibid., 51.

[26] Karen Baker-Fletcher and Garth Kasimu Baker-Fletcher, *My Sister, My Brother: Womanist and Xodus God-Talk* (Maryknoll, N.Y.: Orbis, 1997) 149.

[27] Alice Walker, *In Search of Our Mothers' Gardens* (New York: Harcourt Brace Jovanovich,

part of what it means to be a black woman within a womanist theological construction.

Baker-Fletcher's emphases draw out the importance of naming, of relying on Black women's experience, and of the sustaining power of God. She refers to Anna Julia Cooper's statement that "the world needs to hear all of women's voices across color lines . . . ."[28] Her guiding question attempts to discern how Black women in particular reflect and share in God's creative and sustaining activity.[29] I will quote at length her introduction of the seven emphases:

> *faith*, which has to do with the power of belief in a God of infinite possibilities for fulfillment in creation; *voice*, which has to do with the power of prophetic speech and naming; *survival*, which includes gifts of healing, resistance against evil, 'making do,' and 'making a way out of no way'; *vision*, which has to do with prophetic sight; *community building*, a form of social salvation and healing; *regeneration*, which requires memory and the passing on of wisdom, knowledge for survival, healing, and liberation; and *liberation*, acts of struggle for freedom and social reform.[30] [emphasis mine]

These metaphors for creative participation with God taken together—faith, voice, survival, vision, community building, regeneration, liberation—draw out the need for women to speak from their particular experience for the purpose of liberation and new life. Individually, they present the ways in which the full humanity and agency of black women is developed and affirmed.

"Faith" is simply presented as belief in God—the belief that God presents continuous possibility for fulfillment in the world, for the transformation of creation. This understanding of faith is inevitably hopeful as Baker-Fletcher presumes the belief in a God who empowers the world, and who shares power with believers. She refers to a connection with process theology which this understanding of faith and God presents, and we will see that fleshed out in the section on connections with process thought below.

Using one's "voice," naming one's experience is described here as prophetic. Naming the present and envisioning the future requires a specific understanding of the human being as active agent of her own reality. Transformation and salvation in this understanding depend upon the participation of each person in the community, fully and authentically. The struggle for freedom encompasses both the dominant religious and social situations in

---

1983) xi.
[28] *My Sister, My Brother*, 151.
[29] Ibid., 150.
[30] Ibid., 149.

which African-American women live their lives, and for that reason, women must find and employ their own voices in order to address the church and the world, critically and proactively.

"Survival" and "making a way out of no way" are tied to the history of Black women, and are particularly traced through scripture and the story of Hagar in the work of Delores Williams. Baker-Fletcher depends upon Williams for the development of this concept, and maintains the connection between survival and quality of life that indicates "a form of survival that includes healing, wholeness, community building, and faith."[31] Speaking of human life in this manner leads one to first affirm and support the things needed for basic sustenance/survival, and then to affirm and support those things which contribute to quality of life/survival, things like safety, fulfillment, love, and trust.

"Survival requires vision," and like voice, "vision" is prophetic, as it has the power to effect a new reality. The gift of resistance enables Black women to both reject those things which destroy human life and to actively participate in those things which give life to future generations. Again dependent upon Williams, Baker-Fletcher shows how the wilderness experience which is characteristic of African-American women's experiences requires hope for survival. To find a way out of the wilderness, one must be able to have both the sight/vision of the past and the hope/vision for a future life.

"Community building" is for the purposes of regeneration and liberation in this proposal. This is where the creative energy of African-American women come into direct social relevance. Referring to the Black church and community, Baker-Fletcher discusses how women have the effect of tar or glue to hold things together. The sacredness of this quality must be recognized and lifted up in order to further enable a valuation of Black women's experiences. If we can affirm with Baker-Fletcher that "they embody what Christians might call the power of *koinonia*,"[32] then we can gain insight as to what human activity makes the difference in communal relationship with God. "Regeneration" and "liberation" are the active components of community building, encompassing both the passing on of life and memory and the struggles that define the African-American community.

"The powers of survival, resistance, and liberation"[33] stand out as the overarching themes of this womanist theological understanding of what it means to be human. With Williams, Baker-Fletcher notes the nature of survival as a daily reality, a sustaining quality throughout the lives of Black

---

[31] Ibid., 152.
[32] Ibid., 154.
[33] Ibid., 159.

women, cradled in a history of survival—both psychic and physical. It is this maintenance within the context of daily struggles that allows the community to continue the struggle for ultimate liberation. We can see the connection with Isasi-Díaz's notion of *la lucha* as characteristic of daily life for Latinas. Baker-Fletcher's womanist construction of what it means to be human embraces the seven aspects of life as a Black woman which she details, acknowledging the reality of history and the present, both in terms of oppression and women's spiritual gifts. The metaphors show the means by which women participate in the creation of a future with the spirit of God.

In keeping with her reassessment of characteristics of being human, she notes the following about a concept of God:

> A classical concept of God as all-powerful perpetuates a subjugative concept of womanhood, humankind, and creation. A concept of God as *most powerful* and as *sharing power*, which emerges from Whiteheadian metaphysics, is in keeping with Christian scriptural concepts of a God who shares gifts of power among the body of believers (1 Cor. 12-14; Eph. 4).[34]

With the above emphases in a discussion of humanity, we can see how the concept of God shifts in terms of power and relationality. We will further explore the connection to Whitehead's thought in a later section of this chapter, but it is important to note here the emphasis on sharing power, and the criticism of omnipotence as it perpetuates the subjugation of humanity, particularly women. Baker-Fletcher attends to the ways in which God shares gifts with the community of believers, and those gifts are gifts of power. The whole human community is gifted with power—and its manifestations are seen in things that she relies upon, like voice and resistance and regeneration. Humans have the capacity to speak, effect transformation, and bring about the future.

Again, we are reminded that capability brings with it responsibility: "God does not exercise sustaining power apart from human responsibility. Humankind is responsible for exercising gifts of vision and sustenance with God."[35] Sharing in God's power brings to mind a co-creation with God. To be human in relationship with God means to have the gift and the responsibility of power. Human agency as we understand it here is connected to, created by, and engendered by God. Baker-Fletcher uses a particular image from Anna Julia Cooper of the human being as "'divine spark' whose source was God—the Creator of all."[36] As the human being needs God in order to

---

[34] Ibid., 148–49.

[35] Ibid., 157.

[36] Ibid., 151.

spark, to receive the gifts of power, God needs the human community and the world in order to effectively exercise power within creation.

The relationship between God and the human being proposed here is nuanced with the image of the creator who infuses creation with the spark of life. This is a spark that enables the human community to exercise its capability and responsibility in bringing about liberation and transformation within the world. The human being in this proposal is embedded in the social and historical struggles of the world. She is likewise capable of "walking to Canada and taking you and a bunch of other slaves";[37] She is capable of tremendous things, including social and individual liberation from literal or psychic enslavement. For Baker-Fletcher, focusing on women's experience within the African-American community leads to a theological affirmation of the presence of God and the advocacy of God for the wholeness of all people. God's power enables human power; therefore God and human beings work together for the well-being of the world.

Mutuality and Sophia

In the context of an extended analysis of the mystery of God, Elizabeth Johnson presents her understanding of the appeal to women's experience and its impact for theology. Her analysis of the human being begins with a recognition of the diversity of women's experience:

> There is no stereotypical norm. Yet living within patriarchal systems does forge among women recognizable experiences of suffering along with typical patterns of coping and victoriously resisting, strategies that enable women to survive.[38]

Recognizable patterns of experience and resistance are what draws the four women theologians examined in this section together. Each offers particular and important analyses of varied dimensions of what it means to be human, but the patterns emerging demonstrate a recognition of struggle, a call for liberation, a criticism of history and dominant traditions, and a retrieval from history of the resources for women's lives and theologies.

Johnson draws out the central importance of mutuality in relationship for feminist theology and ethics. Mutuality is understood as "a relation marked by equivalence between persons, a concomitant valuing of each other, a common regard marked by trust, respect, and affection . . . ."[39] The term "mutual-

---

[37] *In Search of our Mothers' Gardens*, xi.
[38] Elizabeth A. Johnson, *She Who Is: The Mystery of God in Feminist Theological Discourse* (New York: Crossroad, 1992) 61.
[39] Ibid., 68.

ity" appears again in our conversation about the relationship between God and the human being, and Johnson's statement is helpful in understanding what it means. Her statement functions in contrast to attitudes that presume superiority, or the right of domination over against another—attitudes generally reflected in patriarchal ideals. Mutuality, on the other hand, involves trust and valuation of the other, a flow of giving from one to the other and back again. To recall our philosophical base for this project, we find that Johnson affirms how "moral autonomy is grounded on relationship [and] mutuality is a moral excellence . . . ."[40] The tension between that independence which is a critical human characteristic, and the mutuality of relationship that grounds both community and divine/human relations, remains a chief challenge. Independence itself is here grounded within a context of relationality and mutuality. Baker-Fletcher stated a similar position when she said "womanists and feminists in general are concerned with self-actualization and self-love in the midst of a relational understanding of the world."[41]

The context of relationality that is found in community forms a basis for working toward liberation. Johnson speaks of narrative remembrance as an activity that, within human communities, "empower[s] women not as individual monads but in a solidarity of sisters."[42] The point is to be human alongside others, in partnership with others, and also in partnership with God. This kinds of partnering forges bonds across the boundaries of independent selves for the goal of liberation.

> By unleashing a positive type of history, that is, by forming communities of discourse, by engaging together in resistance to oppression and the creative praxis of liberation for all that they cherish, women come to an awareness that they are not nonpersons or half persons or deficient persons, but genuine subjects of history.[43]

Johnson emphasizes discourse (speaking), resistance, and genuine subjectivity. For purposes of this project, we can interpret "genuine subjectivity" to imply the sort of human agency which we are attempting to construct. As opposed to "mere" subjectivity, we can suppose that "genuine subjectivity" actually takes into account the reality of human experience and independence, therefore the activity arising from the person is genuine. Human communities thus have the power to speak about reality, to engage in opposition where there is need, and to transform that reality when necessary. Johnson's feminist

---

[40] Ibid., 69.
[41] *My Sister, My Brother*, 146.
[42] *She Who Is*, 63.
[43] Ibid.

proposal intends to see women realizing their own genuine participation in and responsibility to the community.

Johnson examines the notion of God as Sophia/Wisdom where it is helpful for feminist constructions, and she ultimately relies on some notions from Whitehead's thought. She does this again in contrast to patriarchal theological discourse about God which relies on metaphors of paternity and images of unidirectional power. We have seen how Johnson understands the human being and the human community, and her concept of God therefore relates to a humanity which requires mutuality.

Human agency as we have been trying to discern it finds roots here in Johnson's notions of divine agency. God as Sophia has creative agency, recreative agency, and redeeming agency.[44] Divine power understood in this manner demonstrates energy for making things in the world new, anew, and renewed. Divine relations with the world are therefore defined on the basis of creation.

> Community of life with her [Sophia] enables individuals to arrive at their destiny, and in the end enables the whole world and its history to be rightly ordered in justice and peace.[45]

The relationship of God with the world is here the impetus and strength for both individuals and communities to move toward emancipation and transformation—their destiny. Community with Sophia enables justice, because She is the lure toward justice. In this proposal, justice is the right order of the world, and peace is the appropriate state of affairs.

Johnson's concept of God is Sophia as both embedded in the world, and "transcendent power ordering and delighting the world."[46] Compassion of God for the world is critical for this project. Compassion arises from Sophia's presence within the world, and drives the transcendent power in transformation. God's power must be understood to be compassionate if we are to understand God relating to the world in mutuality. To feel with the world, to feel the world, to feel within the world: these are all characteristics of God as Sophia. Not locating God over against, or even above the world, Johnson demonstrates how this concept is a liberating resource for theology. By understanding God as an invested participant in the world, and humanity as mutual partner dwelling in the world, we can move toward a deeper notion of divine/worldly relations.

---

[44] Ibid., 89.
[45] Ibid., 90.
[46] Ibid., 87.

Johnson's presentation of God proposes divine images grounded in female embodiment for speaking about God. The presentation of power and the images in which that is embodied exemplify that of which we have been speaking: To name reality is to control the conversation. Using a female image for God such as Sophia challenges traditional theological presentations of God as Father, both in presenting an alternate reality and in forcing an admittance that all imagery for God is ultimately subject to human interpretation. It demonstrates that our image of God leads to particular understandings of power, relationship, history and creation of the future. It also points out the power of human interpretation.

Johnson examines several scriptural presentations of Sophia in order to elicit the characteristics which she believes are essential to affirming God as Sophia. Rather than speak of Sophia as a companion of God, or a helper to God, Johnson suggests that we speak of Sophia as God. "Sophia is a female personification of God's own being in creative and saving involvement with the world."[47] This is based on analysis of the work of God and the work of Sophia as presented in the Biblical books of Proverbs and the Wisdom of Solomon, as well as the books of Sirach and Baruch. Sophia as the street preacher in Proverbs 1, 8 and 9 proclaims with her own authority, and "has knowledge, insight, and strength that she wishes to impart; her words are truth."[48] Johnson points out that divine interests lie with justice, truth, and life, and Sophia seeks to order the world accordingly. The three "wisdom poems" to which she refers demonstrate the deity among humanity, challenging humanity and luring humanity toward life.

Johnson uses the text of the Wisdom of Solomon to show personified wisdom at its peak. It is here that the creative, recreative, and redeeming agency takes shape. Sophia is seen working in history through various characters such as Abraham, Moses, and Joseph. Finally, with the Book of Baruch, Johnson discusses Sophia as the divine come to live among humans. All of these stories emphasize the immanence and mutuality of God with the world. The relationship between God and the human being is therefore deeply conditioned when we understand this thorough presence in the world.

The work of God as Sophia is centered around this presence in the world, "inspiring the prophetic word of justice, renewing the earth and the human heart," as well as God/Sophia who is in "solidarity with the one who suffers."[49] As we have seen discussed in several ways, human life is variously characterized by struggle and suffering. To say then that God is fully pres-

---

[47] Ibid., 91.
[48] Ibid., 87.
[49] Ibid., 94, 95.

ent in the world, that Sophia dwells among the people, is to assert that God stands empathetically with those who suffer, even that God suffers. "Speaking about God's suffering can also help by strengthening human responsibility in the face of suffering."[50] The power of such compassionate solidarity can be discerned in human communal relations as well as divine/human relations. This leads eventually into a discussion of Christology and the notion of Jesus-Sophia. We will revisit this notion in our later chapter on Christology.

The power in this language for God, this image of God as Sophia, not only connects with larger feminist theological concerns, but ties into a process theological assessment of the character of God, and the divine role in the world and human life. Johnson utilizes some of these notions herself, and we will now briefly explore the nature of a relationship between feminist theologies and process thought, and allow that conversation to lead us into an examination of the principles of Whitehead's thought that contribute to this theological project.

Connections:
Feminist Theology and Process Thought

In order to connect the previous section with the following section, as well as expand on some connections already made, I will explore briefly the nature of a synthesis between process thought and feminist theology. We have seen how the proposals above utilize some thematic elements regarding the nature of human being and the nature of God. For two of the theologians, Baker-Fletcher and Johnson, the concepts of Alfred North Whitehead play a specific role. The former refers to Whitehead and a process reconstruction of God's power, and the latter refers to the process notion of God as fellow-sufferer when speaking about the compassion of God for the world. More than these particular uses of Whitehead, there are a number of feminist theologians who find in the system of process thought tremendous resource for speaking about God and the world.[51]

Between process thought and feminist theology, common concerns include criticism of classical dualism, abstraction from reality, and separation from experience. "Proponents of feminism and process thought see this dualistic and hierarchical vision of reality as existentially and intellectually inadequate."[52] Each of these schools of thought proposes that the classical

---

[50] Ibid., 267.
[51] See further the work of Rita Nakashima Brock, Anna Case-Winters, Catherine Keller, Mary Grey, and Marjorie Suchocki.
[52] *Feminism and Process Thought: The Harvard Divinity School/Claremont Center for Process Studies Symposium Papers*, edited by Sheila Greeve Davaney, Symposium Series 6 (Lewiston,

tradition has inappropriately and inadequately characterized the human self, the world, and God. The relationships among these characters are likewise faulty. The problems lie in antagonistic dualism and hierarchically valued relationships between elements of any given pair—God over world, individual over community, etc. One is valued over and to the exclusion or ignorance of the other. Process thinkers base their criticism on a reliance on a modern scientific worldview, as feminist thinkers base their criticism on women's experiences of classical dualism and hierarchy.

The constructive elements of these two schools of thought are where further points of convergence lie, and where a synthesis becomes interesting. "[B]oth perspectives begin by affirming the essential subjectivity of all that exists. And both suggest that this subjectivity is essentially social, creative, and processive."[53] We will see the details of a process interpretation of these elements in the following section. We can see how the proposals of the four theologians in the preceding section demonstrate this. To be social is to be an authentic member-participant in the community. This participation is by its very nature creative, in such things as naming reality, giving voice to one's experience, and being an agent of history. The process of life is such that God as Sophia lures the world toward a fuller realization of itself. The concept of static reality is largely absent from these theologies, indeed it would appear to be antithetical to the proposals we have examined. A metaphysical expression of this is found in the philosophy of Whitehead and theological interpretation of it is found in process theologians.

One element shared by process and feminist thought is way in which priority is given to the datum of experience. For feminist theologians, women's experience is taken as primary source and norm. We saw in the four proposals above that attention to women's experience of themselves, the world, and God allows a theologian to draw upon resources and interpretations previously unheard or unexamined. A person can never stand outside of his or her experience, and thus it is an inescapable element in any theological criticism or construction. Moreso, experience is a valuable and provocative source for theology. Within process thought, experience is taken as the key building block of the entire world. To experience is to be real, to be actual. As we saw in the philosophical introduction to process thought, actualization and process are inescapable characteristics of reality. In this section, we will encounter some process theologians who build upon these emphases on experience, relationality, and the relationship between God and the world.

N.Y.: Mellen, 1981) 2.

[53] Ibid., 3.

The understandings of experience function in different ways for feminist theology and process thought. Process theology presumes an ability to stand outside of experience, to examine it in detail of its processes as if one were removed from it. On the contrary, feminist theology insists that one cannot be removed from one's experience of the social location. The very ability to talk about something immediately suggests a removal from it. However, the cognition of experience, the ability to say "I experience thus and so," does not mean that one no longer experiences thus and so. For purposes of the synthesis between process thought and feminist theology, we may think of it this way: Our embeddedness in experience defines the way in which we can discuss what it means to be human, and our ability to engage in the exercise of theological anthropology presumes both this embeddedness and some measure of cognitive perspective. We understand that what we say about experience, about the processes of actualization and becoming, is conditioned by the experiencer from whom those statements arise. As wholly embedded in experience, and as dependent upon it for theological resource, we are called upon to understand it in the best manner possible. Process thought offers an excellent perspective from which feminist theologians can further engage in studying experience and evaluating it as resource for theological proposals.

Process Theological Cosmology: Whiteheadian Principles and Theological Proposals

Now we can move toward further examination of Whitehead's principles and some theological proposals that have arisen out of them: Paul Sponheim's relational theology, Marjorie Suchocki's reconstruction of sin and the God/World relationship, and Catherine Keller's proposal for understanding the human self. These theologians relate conceptually to the feminist proposals we have already seen. More importantly, they directly rely upon Whitehead's thought as it helps to understand the human being, God, and the relationship between them. Before moving to these theological proposals, we will look directly at some components of Whitehead's writing that ground the theological proposals that will follow. This builds upon the philosophical introduction to process thought in the preceding chapter and provides the entrée to theological reflection.

Alfred North Whitehead

Whitehead's philosophy and its theological implications have tremendous depth and breadth. For purposes of this chapter, I am focusing on the elements which feed into the cosmology developed in part five of *Process and Reality*, his *magnum opus*. This includes, in particular, his development of experience as the process of actualization, the reality of ideal opposites, and the presentation of God and the world.

"The connectedness of things is nothing else than the togetherness of things in occasions of experience."[54] Occasions of experience form the basis for relation as it is understood in Whitehead's philosophy. That experience is an "occasion" is what is critical to this being known as "process" thought. It is important to note that both relationship and independence play critical roles for Whitehead, as they both characterize existence, human life, and social reality. The connectedness of things is rooted in the processes of experience in the world.

Experience occurs in the process called concrescence. Concrescence (becoming concrete and emerging) involves processes at both micro- and macrocosmic levels. Regarding the term, Whitehead says: "Concrescence is useful to convey the notion of many things acquiring complete complex unity. But it fails to suggest the creative novelty involved."[55] This process is the creation of complex unification, but it is decidedly more than the mere aggregation of elements into a whole. Rather it is a dynamic process through which novelty and new expressions of life come to fruition. "The many become one, and are increased by one."[56] Where unification and connectedness make the many into one, creativity and novelty guide the increase by one, as the many acquire newness and character. The process moves elements "from disjunction to conjunction."[57] In the moments of human experience, the process is such that past decision, objective reality of the past, and location limit the possibilities open for actualization, and at the same time provide for its novelty and creative self-determination. Therefore, the manner in which an actual entity becomes constitutes its being.

At various times, I have imaged the process of concrescence in different terms and images. In general terms, the process moves from the sheer facticity of the past, to the presence of eternal objects, to the subjective form modifying the physical past, to propositions, to intellectual feeling, to its subjective form, to conclusion/concrescence, and then to superjection. It can be imaged as a series of arrows (> > > > > >) or a series of spirals (@ @ @ @ @ @). The arrow imagery presents a much more linear abstraction of the process, and can help when one specific concrescent moment is broken down into its stages of becoming, from the physical facticity of the past to the influence

---

[54] Alfred North Whitehead, *Adventures of Ideas* (New York: Macmillan, 1933, 1961) 233.

[55] Ibid., 236.

[56] Alfred North Whitehead, *Process and Reality: An Essay in Cosmology* (New York: Macmillan, 1929, 1978) 21.

[57] Ibid.

of eternal objects (unchanging elements of reality), the initial aim (proposal for best possibilities), intellectual feeling (independent appropriation of the former), subjection form and concrescence (decision regarding the present moment) and superjection state (influence of the decision on the world, now as object with influence on all future occasions). The spiral imagery, however, is more appropriate as it helps illustrate the process of becoming as a series of discrete moments that ebb and flow continuously. Concrescence continuously occurs, and therefore is largely preconscious, ultra-rapid, and perhaps even jumbled.

"But to be actual is to be a process. Anything which is not a process is an abstraction from process, not a full-fledged actuality."[58] All aspects of process thought build from this foundation. Understanding experience in process thought starts here, and understanding relationship in process thought starts here. It also enables us to speak of the relationship between the past and the present, between givens and creativity. "Thus perishing is the initiation of becoming. How the past perishes is how the future becomes."[59] Objective reality, that sheer facticity of the past, always informs our present subjective experience; therefore the past and the present situation are integrated into expressions of the future. Those moments of decision that have already occurred determine in limited fashion the possibilities available for future decision. Once decision is made, the moment perishes, and this occurs in perpetuity.

> The true method of discovery is like the flight of an aeroplane. It starts from the ground of particular observation; it makes a flight in the thin air of imaginative generalization; and it again lands for renewed observation rendered acute by rational interpretation.[60]

The creative elements of decision and intellectual feeling, and the influence of decision in its objective state on the future, are key in understanding the notion of freedom and capability within the world. Because the individual has the power to creatively determine for herself in continuous processes of becoming the way in which components will come together, the way that they will relate, she has freedom in determining actuality. This is why togetherness is even more than the "complex unity" of an aggregate. "[*H*]*ow* an actual entity *becomes* constitutes *what* that actual entity *is*."[61] It is crucial to understand here that the process is as important (if not more so) than

---

[58] John B. Cobb Jr. and David Ray Griffin, *Process Theology: An Introductory Exposition* (Philadelphia: Westminster, 1976) 14.
[59] Whitehead, *Adventures of Ideas*, 238.
[60] Ibid., 5.
[61] Whitehead, *Process and Reality*, 23.

the actualized decision. Decisions made become fodder for other processes, because within the process of becoming, decisions made inform the future as objective reality. Decision is here being used in a non-personal manner, to signify that moment at which any actual entity comes to the moment of concrescence. This is when the entity synthesizes the givens and the locations of reality and the past in accord with whatever will the entity has. Freedom is an essential characteristic of decision, and Whitehead insists that levels of reality possess differing degrees of freedom, as we mentioned in the previous chapter. My plants, my cats, and I all possess differing degrees of freedom in part based on the fact of what we are.

From this basic understanding of the process of concrescence that characterizes experience, and that underlies all actuality, we can move to Whitehead's specific presentation of Ideal Opposites. As contrasts, elements of experience often stand in paradoxical relationship to one another. "The chief danger to philosophy is narrowness in the selection of evidence."[62] In order to avoid this danger, we are implored to account for things and ideals in their opposing natures not as they hinder one another, but as they foster the development of the other. The relationship between ideals ought not be antagonistic, rather it ought to be seen as mutually definitive. Indeed the nature of reality is such that opposing realities must be accounted for: "Philosophy may not neglect the multifariousness of the world—the fairies dance, and Christ is nailed to the cross."[63]

The world, in its unity of connectedness, is characterized by diversity and complexity: At the very same time we have the joy of imagination wherein we see fairies dancing in a meadow or benefit from the grace of God, we are confronted with the horrors of execution and a human proclivity to violence. To set each in a context of existence with the other allows an exploration of the roles they play in the constitution of the world. Likewise, Whitehead discusses permanence and flux, order and novelty, as elements of reality that need each other for interpretive measure.

> Permanence can be snatched only out of flux; and the passing moment can find its adequate intensity only by its submission to permanence. Those who would disjoin the two elements can find no interpretation of patent facts.[64]

Order depends on that which novelty explodes—repetition, and novelty as the introduction of new character depends on the dissolution of order.

---

[62] Ibid., 337.
[63] Ibid., 338.
[64] Ibid., 338.

However, each element of a pair of Ideal Opposites finds the limits of its own nature and its relationship to the world in its other. Since Whitehead sees himself as a part of the European philosophical tradition that is a "series of footnotes to Plato," we can identify his indebtedness to the philosopher when he states that "Plato found his permanences in a static, spiritual heaven, and his flux in the entanglement of his forms amid the fluent imperfections of the physical world."[65] Ideal Opposites are inescapable elements of the process that is reality.

The point of introducing Whitehead's conception of Ideal Opposites in this section is not only to lead to the ultimate pair, God and the World, but to expose the nature of relationship in the world where it would seem to be the most disjointed. The point is not to insist on happy unification of all things in opposition, nor to insist on definition by opposition, rather it is to insist on an understanding of reality which involves and creates things that exist in disjunction. The process that is reality depends on the diversity and the movement between opposing elements of the world, and the process is the unifying factor of reality. Relationship is fact.

As I mentioned, God and the World constitute the ultimate Ideally Opposite pair. The relationship between the two is such that they depend on one another for full realization. "They embody the interpretation of the cosmological problem in terms of a fundamental metaphysical doctrine as to the quality of creative origination, namely, conceptual appetition and physical realization."[66] God serves as the former and the World exists as the latter, each gaining completion and fulfillment from the other. This is not to say that the world has no capacity for conceptualization, or that God has no physical component. In fact those elements of these two characters find development through the relationship with the other. Regarding the relationship between them, Whitehead states what we have already seen affirmed from the feminist theologians in this chapter: God "is not *before* all creation, but *with* all creation."[67] As the chief exemplification of what Whitehead calls the metaphysical first principles, God is located within reality, not exempt from it, transcendent to it, or removed from it. This panentheism allows us to blur the boundaries between God and the world, to understand the intimate ways in which the two relate, existing within one another.

As such, God participates in reality as an actual entity which is conceptual appetition. God "is the lure for feeling, the eternal urge of desire."[68] For

---

[65] Ibid., 209.
[66] Ibid., 341.
[67] Ibid., 343.
[68] Ibid., 344.

each moment of creation, God presents possibility in the form of initial aims that guide and ideally persuade the process of actualization. The notion of a purpose, grounded in and guided toward God plays out in this presentation. The idea that God lures the world is metaphysically grounded in the notion that experience, as the basis for reality, is a process through which actual entities move, prehending the past and the present, creatively responding to the potential, and actualizing movement toward the future. The impetus for truth, beauty, and goodness, Whitehead's identified aesthetic principles, comes from God. "He is the poet of the world, with tender patience leading it by his vision of truth, beauty, and goodness."[69] It is the conceptual harmonization of God which frames the movement of the diverse and complex world toward this vision.

> The theme of Cosmology, which is the basis of all religions, is the story of the dynamic effort of the World passing into everlasting unity, and of the static majesty of God's vision, accomplishing its purpose of completion by absorption of the World's multiplicity of effort.[70]

This statement is packed with essential statements about the character of God, the nature of the world, and the dynamic of the relationship between the two. In order to understand Whitehead's presentation, I believe that we must see the individual characteristics of God and the world, according to the construction offered throughout this section of the text. They mutually require one another for completion and fulfillment of their respective existences, because they are different. God's vision and unity find harmony with the world's multiplicity of efforts. Each finds the ultimate in the other. This maintains the dynamism of reality which is characterized by process. "Either side can only be explained in terms of the other."[71] Whitehead insists that each, unity of vision and multiplicity of effort, is equally constitutive of reality.

Connecting this discussion with that of Johnson's concept of God as Sophia, we are able to speak more completely of God in a manner which emphasizes transformation, guidance, mutual relationality with the world, and com-passion. The notion of feeling and suffering with the world is also something which Whitehead picks up when he speaks of God as "the fellow-sufferer who understands."[72] Johnson relied on this notion of God in her final analysis of God as Sophia. In the context of this project, the notion is critical

---

[69] Ibid., 346.
[70] Ibid., 349.
[71] Ibid., 347.
[72] Ibid., 351.

because of its implications for human action in the face of evil and suffering. "Speaking about God's suffering can also help by strengthening human responsibility in the face of suffering."[73] The notion of compassionate solidarity comes strongly out of this, for Johnson, as does the importance of human responsibility. As we will see, these concepts are essential for a constructive theological proposal.

Relational Theology

The tandem questions raised by Paul Sponheim in his construction of process theology, or relational theology as he chooses to name his work, have set the tone for a recent feminist theological book: "Where in the world is God?" and "Where in God is the world?"[74] When paired together, these questions get to the very heart of that which we have been discussing: the relationship between God and the world. Sponheim makes relationship the focal point of his explorations in theology, and his discernment of the nuances of relationality between God and the world moves this chapter into the theological depths to which process thought can be taken.

"So who are we? We are beings in relationship. We live on boundaries. If we dig beneath the boundaries of life, we will find relationships."[75] Relationship is a fundamental characteristic of being human. Human life is also characterized by boundaries, as Sponheim states here, but undergirding those boundaries are relationships. He speaks of both the connectedness and the difference which make up existence, and for our purposes of examining the human being, we see how the tension between individuality and relationship continues to play out.

Sponheim introduces us to a theological reconstruction of the self which focuses on relation with the other. What is said about the self-other relationship connects to what is said about the God-world relationship. In constructing what he terms "relational theology," Sponheim asks the parallel questions above in order to discern elements of the relationship between God and the world. In attempting to "locate" God in the world, we make a statement about God, and in discerning the place of the world within God's existence, we make a critical statement about the world.

> On the one hand, the world derives its importance from God . . . on the other hand, God gains meaning and value from the world. The

---

[73] Johnson, *She Who Is*, 267.

[74] Paul R. Sponheim, *Faith and the Other: A Relational Theology* (Minneapolis: Fortress, 1993) 21. The feminist theological work referred to is Ann Pederson, *Where in the World is God?: Variations on a Theme* (St. Louis: Chalice, 1998).

[75] *Faith and the Other*, 25.

> point is that God is not only here in the world, but in the world in a way that embraces, transforms, and saves the world.[76]

Sponheim's attempt to work from process thought and construct a relational theology opens up this conversation about God and the world and allows us to learn more about the world, the human being, and God. Making a statement about God's presence in the world as Sponheim does above tells us that God is committed, powerful, and compassionate. Likewise, the world is valuable, powerful, and creative.

Within process/relational theology, mutuality is held up as a crucial element of the relationship between God and the world. Relationship within the world is given from God, and is an essential characteristic of what it means to be human.

> This, to be human with the other, is not some secondary word added to a defining common property. At the base, from the beginning, to be human is to be with one who is other.[77]

And since this statement follows on the heels of the affirmation that humans are created in the image of God, a central Christian tenet, relationship becomes understood as critical not only within the world but between God and the world. "That human beings, made in God's image, should need each other is not to be lamented."[78] Creation as an act of God is the primordial act of relationship. If one accepts that God created the world (in whatever manner one understands creation), then one must accept that God wanted the world, wanted to be in relationship with the world, and all that is left to discern is the nature of that relationship. "[I]n creation, God wills to be in relationship, God wills to know otherness. In this there is newness for God . . . ."[79] Life in relationship is to be accepted, celebrated, and lived fully. Sponheim speaks of newness for God and expresses the manner in which the relationship between God and the world brings fulfillment and novelty to the lives of each.

Life in relationship undergirds the boundaries of the self, a notion we encountered when examining implications of Kant's philosophy, which returns in this examination of a relational theology. Within this context of relationality, we must become better equipped to deal with questions of individuality and boundaries of the human self. It is an idea that Catherine Keller specifically picks up on in her feminist theological proposal. It also returns us to the philosophical problem illuminated in the first chapter.

---

[76] *Where in the World is God?* 27.
[77] *Faith and the Other*, 53.
[78] Ibid., 63.
[79] Ibid., 89.

> We certainly cannot quietly insert the same old substantial and static self within the fabric of relatedness we have been describing. The boundaries of the self become softer, for the self in its radical temporality is permeable.[80]

If relatedness is the underlying fabric of existence, we must understand the human self as able to ebb and flow with the dynamic of relationality. To be affected by the other and to affect the other counter the notion of a self which is substance and static. The human self is active, dynamic, and moving with the currents of relationality; its choices and movements affect the movements of others, and vice versa. This is the point where Sponheim's relational theology brings us further into feminist theological construction.

The Relational/Separate Self

Whitehead's contribution for a feminist theological proposal of the self is elaborated by Catherine Keller. She takes issue with the mythical tradition that has informed much of cultural and theological reality and the way in which it presents human beings, male and female, and their ideal characteristics. Her proposal takes seriously the power of fairy tale and myth as they inform our perceptions of who we are.

> As women we know well the cast of Sleeping Beauties, Snow Whites and servile Cinderellas sustaining a mythos of feminine passivity intact through the ages. The imagining of our future has been channeled into a soporific hope for the redeeming prince . . . . His the agency, hers the patience.[81]

She questions why women continue to support such an ideal of self-negation, and proposes that re-thinking the self in accord with some Whiteheadian principles assists us in appropriately understanding what it means to be human.

As we saw in Sponheim, the focus again is relationality. Relationship is fundamental to humanity, to the self. "If we are to insist on the connections, on the intrinsic, that is, essential, connectivity of self, we need a greater theoretical width than psychology permits. Archaic as it may seem, we shall have to get metaphysical."[82] The theoretical to which she ultimately turns is found in Whitehead's thought. It is here that she finds the most effective manner in which to speak about the essential connectivity of the self while preserving

---

[80] Ibid., 64.
[81] Catherine Keller, *From a Broken Web: Separation, Sexism, and Self* (Boston: Beacon, 1986) 15.
[82] Ibid., 155.

its individual integrity. We have seen how process cosmology begins in and depends on the minutiae of experience, in the process of concrescence, and in the formation of actualities. Keller uses this to address the issue of selfhood and women's history of self-negation.

Combining some psycho-theory with her analysis of human development, Keller suggests that "the connected, permeable ego ascribed to female children fits the description of an actual entity, that is, what is really actual...."[83] The actual entity takes in the objective past and prehends it in subjective form, becoming something in accord both with its will and with its influences: The perception of "femaleness" likewise emphasizes that the boundary of the self is somewhat permeable, emphasizing relationship more than individuality, as the female takes in multitudes of things, synthesizing and living out of that reality. The social suppression of this with the overvaluing of the rigid and delineated male ego, she says, has contributed to the detriment of all attempts to understand human becoming. With Whitehead, she proposes that we affirm the interrelatedness of all things, including but not limited to human beings. With this affirmation, she shows how this ontological or cosmological statement provides us with a "valuable obliqueness . . . [which] allows us to reconsider the self without plunging into self-objectification."[84]

She proposes that we think in terms of a distinction between the self and the person. Simply put: the person is, and the self becomes. "Person" is here understood as the unification of all past, present, and future decisions and actions; it is the enduring character. "Self" is that which continues to ebb and flow, to change and come to fruition and start over again. The self is the "I," always the present state of being; the person is the continued character of existence and all that is associated with "me." Whitehead saw the person as a form of society in terms of the interrelated actual entities within. Keller suggests: "Everything, and most intimately my soul, flows in and out of the present occasion, which is my self. This is a light and loose sense of the unity of the person."[85] Here we get a picture of the permeability of self, with the continuity of history tied to the person. Any attempt to hold fast to one rigid identity is bound to fail, as there is an essential need for dynamism, the influx and outpouring of feeling. She relies on images of water -- oceanic currents, streams flowing into rivers. The "I" continually changes as the present moment continually changes, but that which is "me" endures and take shape through time.

---

[83] Ibid., 189.
[84] Ibid., 194.
[85] Ibid., 197.

The value of Keller's proposal lies in her development of the human self as a dynamic, permeable, and creative being. This is a helpful way to think about the creative agency which is a part of being human, and she offers a means by which to speak of both relationality and individuality. She offers it in correction to traditions which overvalue static identity, separateness, and definite human constructions of the self which disallow or underappreciate such movement and solubility within the structures of the world. She uses Whitehead as he shows how the processes of becoming and concrescence characterize the general nature of reality, and she synthesizes this with a feminist construction of the self in particular. If the rhythms of life are to be found within the character of the world, then they find intense expression within the becoming of the human self. She finally asserts that a notion of God, and any metaphors for the divine employed by feminist theologians, will have to "imply the metaphysics of cosmic relativity."[86] Further implications of this are drawn out in analyses of Christian doctrine, as in the next section.

Sin and Well-being in the World

Relationship forms the thematic connection between the three theologians introduced in this section. Like Sponheim, Marjorie Suchocki turns toward speaking of "relational theology" as an effective way to express the synthesis between process and feminist theologies. " 'Process' denotes the dynamism of existence, and assuredly implies this relational essence."[87] She takes the idea of relationality seriously in terms of God's relationship to the world, and the world's activity as it affects God. One of her particular concerns is to explore the inadequacies of a traditional Christian notion of sin, and the ways in which relational theology can contribute to a more appropriate constructive proposal.

It would appear to be a simple question that Sponheim raised: where in the world is God? I posed the question to a classroom of second-year seminary students, and the first jovial response was "Everywhere!" If this is in fact the case, then we have already reached the core of Suchocki's proposal. She engages in a critical analysis of Christian traditional conceptions of God as transcendental ruler in relation to the world, and the definitions of "sin" that have arisen from there.

> Since God is the only proper determiner of one's place and conduct, actions that trespass God's will are by definition sin, and more spe-

---

[86] Ibid., 214.
[87] Marjorie Hewitt Suchocki. *The Fall to Violence: Original Sin in Relational Theology* (1994; reprinted, Eugene, Ore.: Wipf and Stock, 2003) 48n.

cifically, the sin of pride.... [I]ts foundations rest in the defiance of limits set by God, and hence in defiance of God.[88]

Concerned primarily with the work of St. Augustine and Reinhold Niebuhr, Suchocki characterizes a traditional concept of sin fundamentally as sin against God. This presumes that God sets the limits of acceptable activity, as the lawmaker and enforcer, so to speak. The human being is primary offender in the realm of God's rule, and therefore is to be somehow punished and humbled. Whether or not this is an oversimplification of Christian traditional thought regarding sin, the point is that the human being in this respect is generally understood as wholly other than God, and the relationship between the two has this radical differentiation in it.

Suchocki's proposal is that we think of sin not as transgression of boundaries set by the divine, or rejection of the gifts bestowed by God, but as a violation of the well-being of creation. "Sin as the unnecessary violation of the well-being of any aspect of creation ... indicates not a primacy of one being against another, but a primacy of the well-being of all, against which one rebels in sin."[89] The move is to locate sin, human activity, directly within creation, and as violation it is thus against creation. This helps us to deal adequately with the consequences of sin, as it prioritizes inter-worldly relations. It brings us back to the question of God within process and feminist theologies because God is understood to be immanent in the world. Therefore, any violation of creation is a violation of God. God feels all that the world feels, and this "fellow-sufferer who understands" is affected by what happens in the world. It is important to note that it happens in the world, and *therefore* it happens to God. God is not removed from the picture, rather is relegated to a relational status with regard to the world's activity.

Suchocki's argument for redefining sin in this manner most importantly allows appropriate responsibility to be assigned for sin as violation of well-being, and it also allows us to deal with the concrete effects of that violation in the world. Since sin is primarily against creation, we must therefore attend to the healing of creation. When we speak of sin as primarily against God, then we create a false distinction between the well-being of the world and the well-being of God. Affirming the value of creation alongside our confessed human failings preserves and protects creation at all levels—social, ecological, spiritual—and it creates space in which we can attempt to move toward healing and redemption with God as a partner in the processes of the world.

This theological proposal integrates much of what we have gleaned thus far from feminist and process theologies. It attends to the inherent relational-

---

[88] Ibid., 29.
[89] Ibid., 48.

ity of existence, speaks of God as fully present in the world, deals with the concrete consequences of human activity, and affirms the ability of the human community to make a difference in the world, working in relationship with God.

> What we do know is that God has acted and does act for us in Jesus Christ, that this reality we name God undergirds and supports us, judges and redeems us, and calls us to wider circles of caring for the well-being of creation.[90]

Concluding Remarks

"Feminist" theological proposals for understanding God and the human being, combined with process theological cosmology, form the contemporary base from which we will move to examine traditional resources for the same conversation found in Luther. We have seen how these contemporary theological proposals lift up some themes in varying ways: relationality and freedom, responsibility and agency, creativity and capability as characteristic of the human being; solidarity and Sophia, creativity and a liberating vision as characteristic of God; struggle, partnership, novelty, and action as characteristic of the relationship between God and the human being.

All of these things converge to help us understand the importance of detailing the relationship between God and the world. If it is our hope to look at the critical issues raised in Christology and atonement, we must see the foundation for solutions in theological analysis of the human being and God in relationship. This is because the issues of the Jesus story lie for the most part in the dynamic of relationality between God and the world. A renewed understanding of theological anthropology in this way contributes fresh resources to the conversation. This approach to Christology and atonement then will move us to re-examine the concrete expressions of the relationship found in the sacraments. In order to solve the "problems" of atonement and Christology, we have turned to the fundamental way we view the relationship between God and the human being. These renewals in turn suggest a new way to understand the theology of the eucharist, as a sacrament which concretely manifests the relationship.

We have examined what it means to be human, and to be human in relationship with God in these first two chapters—from the philosophical self to cosmological theology. We will now move to an examination of traditional resources as found in Luther's writings on the sacraments, and what they tell us about these concepts. We will take the contemporary theological

---

[90] Ibid., 53.

proposals from this chapter in particular to elicit the continued impact of Luther's theology. We will further see how Luther stands as a challenge for these theologies, and pushes them to clarify the role of God in the world, and the relationship between humanity and the divine. Resonance and resistance will be encountered, and the implications for our constructive proposals will be drawn out.

3

Finitum Capax Infiniti in Luther's Writings on the Sacraments

WHY are we now moving from particular theological conversation about the human being and God, theological anthropology, to examining elements of sacramental theology?[1] Why Luther's sacramental theology? And why do we move back to traditional resources after locating the project squarely within contemporary schools of thought like feminist theologies and process thought?

Within Christian expression of the relationship between God and the human being, the sacraments are affirmed to be concrete manifestations of that relationship. They do this in the moments, the time and space locations, of the sacraments, when Christians affirm something about God, and God acts in the midst of the human community. The faith and theology of the community is publicly and concretely expressed through the activity of the sacraments. What is this and how does this happen? What *is* being said or expressed or affirmed about the relationship between God and the human being in the located time and space of Christian celebration of the sacraments? The answers to those questions will lend a new dimension to speaking about and understanding the relationship between God and the human being. In particular, they will further our attempt to lift up human agency within the world and within the divine-human relationship. This all feeds in to our attempts to get to the critical issues of Christology and atonement, related in their own way to sacramental theology.

---

[1] I use the phrases "sacramental theology" and "theology of the sacraments" somewhat interchangeably in this discussion. I mean to indicate that which is being said about the sacraments and the theological implications and rationale surrounding it.

Within the tradition of Christian thought, Luther is not only a pivotal Reformation figure, but is a theologian who located the sacraments at the heart of Christian life. The sacramental system was a prime target of his reforming theology, and he gave detailed attention to the sacraments both in terms of what they express about the Christian community and what they affirm about God's relationship to the human being. His understanding of human life is guided and shaped in part by his understanding of the sacraments of baptism and eucharist. From this, it follows that our conversation about the relationship between God and the human being will gain much from a discussion about the sacraments. Because of Luther's commitment to reforming the sacramental system it makes good sense that a conversation about the sacraments involve Luther. Finally, because of my own commitments, Luther is inevitably a part of the way in which I do theology. The resource and the challenge that Luther's theology provides to this book are both substantive and personal.

The contemporary theological proposals that we have examined thus far will serve this chapter of the book as a sort of critical and appreciative gauge. Likewise, Luther will serve as a critical voice to those proposals which we have examined up to this point. We understand "tradition" from the places in which we presently stand as a part of its trajectory. It has been important to flesh out the contemporary context of this proposal prior to examining its relationship to a theological "tradition" as I find it in Luther. It is important to detail both the contemporary resources and the traditional sources which inform my way of doing theology. Working with them together illumines each in an interesting way.

This examination of Luther's writings on the sacraments regarding the relationship between God and the human being will be influenced by the context out of which it is now moving. While Luther will be read as a critical challenge to our contemporary resources, these theologians will serve as interpretive measure of the appropriateness of what we will find in Luther's thought. How are God and the human being presented in his writings on the sacraments, and how do such proposals relate to what we have seen in contemporary theologies? In what ways is Luther a resource for a constructive project, and in what ways does Luther's presentation no longer appropriately serve the needs of contemporary theological and social perspectives? The point of this chapter is to interpret Luther in light of our present theological concerns, and to see the way in which his presentation of the relationship between God and the human being in his writings on the sacraments can both challenge and inspire our present work.

We will begin this chapter, therefore, by looking specifically at Luther's writings on the sacraments. Along with discerning what Luther says about baptism and eucharist in general, we will look in particular for those things that express something about what it means to be human and what it means for God to be God. We will seek to understand how the sacraments are an expression of the relationship between God and the human being and what the implications of that are for theology today.

The God/Human Relationship in Luther's Sacramental Theology

Martin Luther's reforming theology concerned itself with particular errors of the Roman church—one of which was the authority structures inherent in the papacy, another of which was the sacramental system. Working in the midst of theological and ecclesial political conflict, Luther wrote dramatic treatises explaining and defending his position regarding the specific mechanics and theological implications of the sacraments. Within Christianity, the sacraments were thought to be the very heart of Christian life, and therefore a proper understanding of them was absolutely critical. For Luther, the sacraments were important because they were God's gifts and ways of being present with the individual and the community. It was over sacramental theology that Luther found himself in deepest conflict with the dominant Roman church and other contemporaries. He fought for the integrity of the sacraments of baptism and eucharist so that no external authority like the papacy denied or interfered with the individual Christian's relationship with God.

I will look at his texts on both baptism and eucharist here, as there are thematic elements present in Luther's sacramental theology that speak to the anthropological issues we are exploring. His assertions about the sacraments of baptism and eucharist, their intent and their nature, make statements about what it means for the human being to be in relationship with God. Likewise, his assumptions about the nature of God inform how he theologically constructs and defends sacramental theology. I will focus not on the rubrics that Luther addresses, i.e. administration of the sacraments, but will examine the theology presented in these writings as it pertains to understanding the relationship between God and the human being.

General Principles of Luther's Sacramental Theology

Luther wrote in opposition to the prevailing official theology of his time. This adversarial context forms much of what and how he writes, although he remains fundamentally concerned with the sanctity of the Christian soul. He proposed that some basic differences exist between what God intended for the community of believers, and what the Roman church insisted constituted a church. For Luther, the key characteristic of the *Gemeinde*, the community, was the centrality of word and sacrament:

> Now, wherever you hear or see this word preached, believed, professed, and lived, do not doubt that the true *ecclesia sancta catholica*, 'a Christian holy people' must be there, even though their number is very small.[2]

In speaking about the marks of the church, Luther starts with the importance of the word, and then discusses the sacraments of baptism and the eucharist. The other marks of the church include the power of the keys and the ritual of what we call ordination. It is important to note here that word and sacrament center all things for the community of believers. Preaching the word, hearing the word, and participating in the word through the sacraments within the community constitute Christian life for Luther. Word and sacrament signify the presence of God and the commitment of the community to God.

The word of God, therefore, forms the basis of the authority of the church. Even the power of the sacraments is drawn in part from the word. Luther used his study and interpretation of scripture as the word of God to challenge the claimed authority of the Roman church, and to demonstrate the ultimate authority of the word. His general principle of *sola scriptura* assumes that all things can and ought to be found in and through scripture. Scripture alone is the criterion by which matters of spiritual concern are to be judged. "Thus the pure truth of the gospel gives genuine authority to the men of the church who witness to Christ."[3] Luther did not seek to abolish the authority of the papal church, rather he intended to relegate it to its proper limited realm, dependent upon the word of God for authentication. He then used his understanding of the gospel for his theological defense of various issues within the church, including the sacraments.

In the life of a Christian, the word of God is the tool by which a person can gauge the appropriateness of worldly authorities:

> When a man-made law is imposed upon the soul to make it believe this or that as its human author may prescribe, there is certainly no word of God for it. If there is no word of God for it, then we cannot be sure whether God wishes to have it so . . . .[4]

---

[2] Martin Luther, "On the Councils and the Church," (1539) in *LW* 41:150.

[3] Paul Althaus, *The Theology of Martin Luther*, trans. Robert C. Schultz (Philadelphia: Fortress, 1966) 340.

[4] Luther, "Temporal Authority: To What Extent it Should be Obeyed," (1523) in *LW* 45:105.

The word of God is the gauge by which individuals can judge the appropriateness of human laws and proscriptions. This informs his approach to the sacraments: if there is no word of God for a law imposed by the church, then it has no true authority. For Luther, the power of the word of God to establish and inform the community is central to his understanding of the sacraments.

Luther speaks of the sacraments as that element of Christianity where the word of God is most powerfully definitive, and the element where the authority of the papacy has overstepped its limits most horribly. His analysis maintains that there are not seven sacraments as the Roman church believes, but eventually only two.[5] This assessment is based on the need for both word and sign—promise and element. We will see how his writings on the sacraments deal with the relationship between the world and the word of God. The importance of both the physical sign and the spiritual significance is crucial to the development of his thought.

This relationship between the physical and the spiritual takes on particular character within the scope of his thought when Luther argues *finitum capax infiniti*: the finite is capable of the infinite, or the finite can hold the infinite. This is not a concept at all limited to his sacramental theology, but it is one that is a part of his discussion of the sacraments. This plays an important role in understanding his theology of the eucharist, as we will see. As a general axiom describing his thought, however, it is important here that we explicate this theme of relationship between finite and infinite, physical and spiritual, the human being and God, element and word. It is important to see that Luther affirms the physical and finite existence of the world in a way that makes it capable and "worthy" of holding or possessing the infinite and the divine. This is a thoroughly incarnational line of thought: It is only when the finite is capable of the infinite that God can be present in the world in the person of Jesus. It is through the physical reality of his being, the embodiedness within the world, that we experience God. Likewise, it is in the finite moments of the sacraments that we express and experience publicly and deeply our infinite connection to God. Word and sacrament are inextricably bound for Luther in part because the finite and the infinite have been irreversibly brought together by God in Christ through the word, in the world, experienced in the sacraments. This marked affirmation of the physical, the finite, distinguished Luther's thought from that of many contemporaries.

In the written pieces of his pastoral trilogy of 1519 on the sacraments (in which at that time he still included penance), Luther spells out the three

---

[5] For the sustained argument about the number of sacraments, see Martin Luther, "The Babylonian Captivity of the Church," (1520) in *LW* 36:3–126.

main elements that constitute a sacrament: the sign (finite), its significance (infinite), and the faith (personal) with which it is received. In baptism and eucharist, the sign enables the physical participation and the particular way in which God comes to us. Baptism involves a sign of water as death and rebirth, and the eucharist exists with a sign in the bread and wine as the body and blood of Jesus. The significance of each will be examined in depth in the following sections, and generally each finds its significance in the word of promise spoken by God through Jesus Christ. The faith with which the sacraments are received make the benefits of communion with God personal, *pro me*, for me. While Luther affirms that it is God who acts, the significance and sign of the sacrament are engaged only when they are received in faith.

> Luther's notion that God is present 'for us' in the Word and sacraments is the gospel's corrective to the . . . simplistic, universal message that says nothing particular to the hearts of specific believers.[6]

While the word is preached for all to hear, the sacraments are individual activities whereby the individual both expresses her faith and receives the gifts given to her by God. For Luther, word and sacrament enable, sustain, and express faith.

Luther's sacramental theology is the locus of his thought which concretely expresses the relationship between God and the human being. "As the word itself, so the sacrament is always God's personal encounter with man."[7] Word and sacrament are intimately bound together for Luther: where there is one there is the other. It is important that the promise be connected with the sign: the infinite with the finite. In general, Luther's sacramental theology presents the human being as related to God through promise and commitment, and sets up the necessity for death and rebirth as a cycle of renewal. Promise and commitment, faith and grace operate in this conversation to illumine Luther's understanding of what it means to be a human being in relationship to God.

When speaking about the presence of Christ, particularly in the eucharist, Luther refers to three different modes of being present: "circumscriptively, definitively, repletively."[8] Our understanding of the presence of God can thus be nuanced with these distinctions. This is one way in which Luther illustrates the power of God who, while working in the world, is not limited by the sense of human beings to comprehend exactly what is happening. "It

---

[6] Ann Pederson. *Where in the World is God? Variations on a Theme* (St. Louis: Chalice, 1998) 120.

[7] Althaus, *The Theology of Martin Luther*, 348–49.

[8] Luther, "Confession Concerning Christ's Supper," (1528) in *LW* 37:215.

transcends nature and reason, even the comprehension of all the angels in heaven, and is known only to God."[9]

The first way of being present is local presence: "space and object correspond exactly."[10] This would correspond to Jesus' presence in the world as a human being. It can be seen and measured and touched. The second way Luther calls the mode of angels or demons and likens to possession. In this mode, there is a space occupied by the thing, but it is not space to be measured or to correspond with space as we understand it. This is how Luther comprehends Christ's body as he came out of the tomb. The third way is "simultaneously present in all places whole and entire, and fills all places, yet without being measured or circumscribed by any place."[11] This is the way in which Christ is present in the sacraments. It is the mode relying wholly on faith. The point of this is to lift up the incomprehensibility of the ways in which God works in the world. Human reason cannot bind an understanding of God's work and presence in the world. The sacraments are instances in which God works in the world: "Who will be so bold as to measure and span the power of God . . . ?"[12]

We will attempt to lift out anthropological themes in this sacramental theology which will in turn serve in renewing our understanding of some of the key issues in this project. What is Luther's sacramental theology telling us about what it means to be human, and to be in relationship with God? What does he assert about God? And what difference does it make for contemporary theological proposals?

Baptism

Baptism, for Luther, is essentially the death to sin and rebirth of the human being in the name of God, in faith. "The significance of baptism is a blessed dying unto sin and a resurrection in the grace of God, so that the old man, conceived and born in sin, is there drowned, and a new man, born in grace, comes forth and rises."[13] The German word that Luther uses is *die Taufe* which he relates to the word *tief*, deep. The Greek word he cites is *baptisma*, which means immersion. He suggests that these words express something fundamental about baptism: To be baptized is to be immersed deep into the water, to be drowned to an old life, to be taken to the depths of humanity, and to be raised up out of the deep, resurrected into a new life with Christ.

---

[9] Ibid., 223.
[10] Ibid., 215.
[11] Ibid., 216.
[12] Ibid., 217.
[13] Luther, "The Holy and Blessed Sacrament of Baptism," (1519) in *LW* 35:30.

This connection suggests that immersion be the fullest expression of what is occurring in baptism, though it is not always the practical expression. But because he speaks so vividly of death unto sin and being born in grace, immersion in the water and coming out in resurrection to life in Christ become appropriate forms of baptism.

Embedded in this basic statement about the sacrament are several assertions about human nature. Human beings are discussed as they are born of sin, and born into sin. There is a connection between human fleshly life and sinful nature. Therefore, human beings need to die to this old life. The first birth is that of the flesh and from the flesh—in sin (*fleischlich geburt ein sundigs mensch*). The second birth is spiritual and brings a person into life with Christ.

> For just as a child is drawn out of his mother's womb and is born, and through this fleshly birth is a sinful person and a child of wrath, so one is drawn out of baptism and is born spiritually. Through this spiritual birth the person is a child of grace and a justified person.[14]

Baptism, therefore, is a rebirth, a second birth, a spiritual birth (*auß der taufe geholen und geborn der mensch geistlich*) brought about by God through the sign of water, with the word of God, the promise. Through this God gifts the person with grace and justice (*der gnaden und rechtfertigs*).[15]

Baptism effects what Luther understands to be justification (*Rechtfertigung*). It is expressed in its complete form: "Baptism, then signifies two things—death and resurrection, that is, full and complete justification."[16] To be made righteous before God, the person must go through this death to the old life and embrace new life with the resurrected Christ. Baptism marks the beginning of faith, and, Luther says, the beginning of our death to the world.

There exist, in principle, two characters in this understanding of the life of a Christian: the old person who lived in sin, and the new person who is born in the word of God through the sacrament of baptism. "A baptized person is therefore sacramentally altogether pure and guiltless."[17] Through spiritual rebirth via the word of God in Christ, the person is made sacramentally righteous and therefore begins the life of communion with Christ. Although the person remains human, and therefore a sinner, Luther claims that the new life granted through baptism is given by God for the fulfillment of the word.

---

[14] Ibid., 30.

[15] German text from "*Ein Sermon von den heiligen Hochwirdigen Sacrament der Taufe.*" (1519) *D. Martin Luthers Werke. Kritische Gesammtausgabe* (Weimar: Hermann Bohlau, 1884) 2:728

[16] Luther, "The Babylonian Captivity of the Church," (1520) in *LW* 36:67.

[17] "The Holy and Blessed Sacrament of Baptism," 32.

God acts to transform the old person into the new, fulfilling the promise in bodily death. Salvation for the person who continues to live in this world, struggling against sin, lies in the grace that sin will no longer control his destiny. "For no sin can condemn him save unbelief alone."[18] In baptism, God's promise is fundamentally that the individual is no longer bound to the eternal effects of sin and that God promises to be with the individual throughout her life and into her death. In bodily death, spiritual renewal deepens and life with Christ takes on fuller form.

Luther emphasizes that it is God who acts in this sacrament, and acts for particular reasons. "This blessed sacrament of baptism helps you because in it God allies himself with you and becomes one with you in a gracious covenant of comfort."[19] God comes to the person; God brings about justification. Luther points out that priests baptize "in the name of" God, and not in their own name. "For I hold that 'in the name of' refers to the person of the Doer . . . ."[20] This is a part of Luther's argument for the limited authority of the papacy and the leadership of the church, since he believes that it needs to be based on the word of God. Although the priest acts in the name of God, it is God who acts to baptize the person. God alone holds that power. This is also crucial for Luther's assertion that the human being is the blessed recipient in the sacrament of baptism and is not a cooperator in any active sense.

The alliance itself is the difference that baptism makes in the life of the believer. While it does remove the person from the effects of punishment for sin, it does not take sin and temptation away. More importantly, it adds something to the life of the person, that is God. In baptism, God comes to the sinner, the individual human being who is in some state of dis-ease. Regardless of merit, in fact despite a lack thereof, God unites with the human being, bringing about comfort through a commitment of alliance. It is God's very presence that is gracious, born of no work or merit on the part of the human being. For this reason, among others, the baptism of infants is acceptable as far as Luther understands it. The family can bring the child to God as expression of their own faith, but God acts in baptism to bring that child into the community of Christ. Even though the human being continues to live enmeshed in a world of sin, God's alliance becomes a gift of strength and security. The individual can then grow within the community into her life of faith. Within the scope of this discussion of infant baptism, the faith of another can serve as the means for the infant to come to faith, but the individual herself must come into her own faith. Likewise, when an adult comes

---

[18] "The Babylonian Captivity," 60.
[19] "The Holy and Blessed Sacrament of Baptism," 33.
[20] "The Babylonian Captivity," 63.

in faith to be baptized, it is God who acts to bring that person into new life with Christ—the person does not bring herself into the eternal community.

God's power and grace is manifest in this moment of expressing the commitment to the human being. This contradicts that which Luther fought against—the Roman teaching that one must work and struggle to become righteous in the eyes of God. Baptism is not something that we do to earn favor in the sight of God. Rather, here it is understood as something that God does to bestow favor upon us. For Luther's adversaries, the radical simplicity of the human response must have been (and indeed it was) troubling. The human does nothing, in fact can do nothing. This was a radical and liberating message for many. It is God who works, through the faith of the community, to bring each new life into fulfillment in Christ. "For faith is a work of God, not of man . . . look upon the person administering it as simply the vicarious instrument of God . . . ."[21] God's power is grace, for Luther, and it fills the sacramental moments with infinite significance.

Life after one's baptism is lived in this public covenant with God. It is something done once which has full effectiveness for the life of the believer. Even if one falls into disbelief or disillusionment, God's grace keeps the promises made in baptism. "Thus, you have been once baptized in the sacrament, but you need continually to be baptized by faith, continually to die and continually to live."[22] The world continues to be a place full of sin and evil, temptation and trial. The human being continues to be a sinner. Faith is the means by which one can return to the comforts and promises made by God in baptism. In remembering one's baptism, the Christian knows that there is an ally and a comfort:

> For this reason no one should be terrified if he feels evil lust or love, nor should he despair even if he falls. Rather he should remember his baptism, and comfort himself joyfully with the fact that God has there pledged himself to slay his sin for him . . . .[23]

When, not if, the human being sins and is tempted, she is encouraged to remember that she has already been brought into life with God—that the old powers of sin and death have no *ultimate* claim on her life. God's presence is constant, despite the attempts of the world which contains and sometimes promotes evil. The struggle is a constant factor in the life of the Christian, but the struggler finds an ally in God and remembers this through remembering her baptism (*taufgedenken*): "*Sondern an sein Taufgedenken und sich der selben*

---

[21] Ibid., 62.

[22] Ibid., 69.

[23] "The Holy and Blessed Sacrament of Baptism," 35.

fröhlich trosten, das Gott sich da verpfänden hatt, ihm sein sund zu Tödten und nit zur verdamnuß...."[24]

Luther speaks of suffering and the daily trials of human life as they function to strengthen the relationship between God and the human. Baptism, he says, "makes all sufferings, and especially death, profitable and helpful, so that they simply have to serve baptism in the doing of its work, that is, in the slaying of sin."[25] Here again, we return to the idea of death to the old corrupt fleshly life, and it is coupled with understanding that suffering remains a factor in the new life as daily tribulations further challenges and strengthens the Christian's commitment to God who provides comfort in the midst of the world. Luther relies on these extremes to make his point that living in the world is a dangerous venture, one which cannot be done on one's own.

The community, the *Gemeinde*, is critical to the preservation of God's word and the participation in the sacraments. Through baptism, the individual becomes a part of the priesthood of all believers. Citing 1 Peter 2:9, Luther says "all of us that have been baptized are equally priests ... we are all priests, as many of us as are Christians."[26] This is a critical component of Luther's understanding of what it means to be human, more specifically what it means to be a Christian. That we are all equally baptized as priests in the community of God forms the basis for his further development of vocation and ministry as one of those chosen vocations. At this fundamental level, all those who are baptized are equally members of the body of Christ.[27]

Luther affirms the notion that in the life of a Christian, baptism is the "first sacrament." He says that "the truth of the promise once made remains steadfast, always ready to receive us back with open arms when we return."[28] It functions as the basis for Christian life and is the first promise made by God to the human being, a promise of presence and of life. As a sort of great equalizer, baptism brings the Christian into communion with God in

---

[24] "*Ein Sermon von den heiligen Hochwirdigen Sacrament der Taufe*," 731. "[R]ather one should remember one's baptism and comfort himself happily that God has pledged to be with him unto death and not to condemn ...." (trans. mine).

[25] Ibid., 39.

[26] "The Babylonian Captivity," 112–13.

[27] The notion of the priesthood of all believers as it emerges out of Luther is the subject of much debate and scholarship. For further provocative analysis, see Cheryl Stewart, "Integrity in the Priesthood of All Believers," and Judah Kiwovele, "An African Perspective on the Priesthood of All Believers," in *Theology and Black Experience: The Lutheran Heritage Interpreted By African and African-American Theologians*, ed. Albert Pero and Ambrose Moyo (Minneapolis: Augsburg, 1988) 170ff, 56ff. See also Philip Hefner, "Basic Elements of the Church's Life," in *Christian Dogmatics*, vol. 2, edited by Carl E. Braaten and Robert W. Jenson (Philadelphia: Fortress, 1984) 227–31.

[28] Ibid., 59.

a manner which cannot be erased or completely forgotten. It also need not be repeated in its sacramental form. In argument against the "Anabaptists," those who would argue for the sole efficacy of a believer's baptism, Luther defends the integrity of baptism as an effective one-time sacrament "done" by God. Forming his argument around the proposal that even faith need not be a requirement for baptism, and that baptism need not be done only when one "comes to faith" (as it is God who infuses the individual with faith through baptism), Luther proposes that the sacrament is an alliance that cannot be broken:

> Our baptism, thus, is a strong and sure foundation, affirming that God has made a covenant with all the world to be a God of the heathen in all the word, as the Gospel says.[29]

The covenant is public, and therefore cannot be denied, and Luther insists that to make baptism contingent on faith is to make it dependent on human works. To those who argue that the only real baptism is one engaged by a believer, he says that faith can be fleeting and uncertain, as it is a human element. To make it a requirement of effective baptism makes God's grace contingent on human works. On the contrary, Luther insists that baptism is a work of God which needs no human assent.

Through baptism and God's alliance, the Christian is enabled to bear suffering, the *Anfechtung*, the process and the trial, which is human life. The sinner lives her new life in the presence of God, *coram Deo*, in relationship to God, in the sight of God, and together they are committed to "slaying" sin. Faith is the way in which the human being expresses her commitment, and it is her response to as well as her gift from God. The significance of this Latin preposition *coram* is lifted up by Gerhard Ebeling as a fundamental facet of Luther's understanding of human ontology. The term itself has meaning in several senses as an adverb: in the presence of, before the eyes of, in the face of, openly, face to face, present, in person, personally. If human life is fundamentally *coram Deo*, it is in the presence of God, in the face of God, in person with God. To be human implies this relationship with God which can be seen as quite intimate.

Coram suggests the power of being in the presence of another, of being in the sight of another, and of being recognized by another. "In it the way in which [the human being] encounters others, others encounter him, and he encounters himself are interwoven."[30] Ebeling says that Luther speaks of human life *coram mundo* (in presence of the world), *coram meipso* (in presence

[29] Luther, "Concerning Rebaptism," (1528) in *LW* 40:252.
[30] Gerhard Ebeling. *Luther: An Introduction to His Thought*, trans. R. A. Wilson (Philadelphia: Fortress, 1964) 196.

of myself), and *coram hominibus* (in presence of other persons). However, it is human existence *coram Deo*, in presence of God, in the encounter with God, in the sight of God, which is most basic. "Baptism clearly articulates that we are not our own: not rights, but relationships mark the Christian life."[31] This relationality is fundamental to Luther's understanding of the human being and her being in the presence of God.

Coram as a facet of existence speaks of the fundamental relationality of all things. The primary encounters drawn from Luther are the human being who encounters the world, the world which encounters her, her relationship to herself, and the relationships she has with other persons. The relationship with God is a defining characteristic of the Christian person. It defines all of the other relationships she has, and it has its basis in the sacrament of baptism. God struggling with the individual throughout her life, the individual turning to God for comfort, and the joint endeavor to slay sin in the world all depend on a strong base of dynamic relationship.

The word *coram* has many angles of definition, all of which have meaning for this project. From living in the presence, the sight, the vision, and the word of God, the human being enhances her life in relation to other human beings, herself, and the world. If we take the notion of being face to face, we can play with the meaning of "vision." To be seen by and seeing another, along with recognizing and being recognized by another, implies relationship. Vision can also mean something more abstract than sight. What if we speak of God's vision as not only God's recognition of us and relationship to us, but as a divine vision—hope, plan, desire for the present and future? What does this imply for human relationship to God? We will return to this notion of human life *coram Deo*: in the presence of God, in relationship to God, and ultimately committed to the vision of God.

Eucharist

The sacrament of the eucharist is the way in which the individual comes with the community to receive the riches of God, as given to the human community by Christ.[32] Like baptism, the eucharist consists of three elements that solidify its place in the life of the Christian church. The sign, significance, and faith enable us to experience the infinite promise of God through finite earthly elements. The sign is the physical element of the eucharist: "Only the bread and wine must be used in eating and drinking, just as the water of

---

[31] Martha Ellen Stortz, " 'The Curtain Only Rises': Assisted Death and the Practice of Baptism," *CTM* 26 (February 1999) 14.

[32] I still remember my confirmation teacher helping us to learn the meaning of grace: God's Riches At Christ's Expense.

baptism is used by immersion or pouring."³³ Luther dealt with opposition to administration of both the bread and the wine to the laity, and asserted that both kinds ought to be given, as both were instituted by Christ, and therefore willed by God.

> Christ did not institute these two forms solitary and alone, but he gave his true natural flesh in the bread, and his natural true blood in the wine, that he might give a really perfect sacrament or sign.³⁴

The fullness of expression is found in the earthly items of bread and wine. The significance behind them is also instituted by Christ.

The fellowship of all the saints constitutes a significance of the eucharist. The sacrament brings God together with the community of believers through the words of Christ. These words of institution become very important for Luther, and we will return to them shortly. In the sacrament which is also rightly called *communio*, Christ and all people are members of one body, partaking in the flesh and blood as it has been commanded. The community created through the sacrament is instituted by the word of God and made real through Jesus Christ. As we saw in baptism, unity with God, through Christ, is the central element of the sacrament of the eucharist. It is a sign from God that the human being is "united with Christ and his saints and has all things in common, that Christ's sufferings and life are his own . . . ."³⁵ Bringing the community together brings all burdens and joys of the community together. God acts in the midst of this according to grace, bestowing the gifts of forgiveness and salvation and eternal life upon each individual.

Faith is once again the third element of the sacrament. In the eucharist, faith makes the promise one's own gift. Faith enables the individual to realize and recognize that the body and blood were shed "for you." "In this sacrament, therefore, man is given through the priest a sure sign from God himself that he is thus united with Christ and his saints and has all things in common [with them]."³⁶ That the body and blood were given for you, and for the forgiveness of sins, is the point of the eucharist, and only faith can fully comprehend this meaning.

The presence of suffering in human life in the world is again addressed by Luther. "Therefore we need the strength, support, and help of Christ and of his saints."³⁷ Evil and adversity, as we have discussed, remain a powerful

---

³³ Luther, "The Blessed Sacrament of the Holy and True Body of Christ, and the Brotherhoods," (1519) in *LW* 35:49.
³⁴ Ibid., 59.
³⁵ Ibid., 52.
³⁶ Ibid.
³⁷ Ibid., 55.

part of human life after baptism. This is part of the *Anfechtung*, the daily trials and turmoil of human life, the process of being in the world, that Luther struggled with personally and theologically. While baptism remains the fundamental promise of commitment to which humans can return, the eucharist becomes the source of daily strength, a physical reminder of God's continuous commitment to human life. "God gives us this sacrament, as much as to say, 'Look, many kinds of sin are assailing you; take this sign . . . take heart and be bold. You are not fighting alone. Great help and support are all around you.'"[38] Again, the emphasis is on God's commitment to ally with the human being as she attempts to life a "godly" life in the world. In addition, the believer finds herself again and again in community within the fellowship of saints through this sacrament. The struggle that occurs in the world is countered by God's gift of the sacrament of the eucharist, a physical reminder of the commitment.

The words of institution as spoken by Jesus Christ become a critical component of how Luther understands the eucharist. Again, the power of the word of God is lifted up. In the synoptic Gospels and in Pauline literature, Jesus is written of as speaking the words: This is my body, which is given for you; This cup is the new testament in my blood; Do this in remembrance of me. Luther draws out these statements over and over again, insisting that they be read literally, definitively. There is both a command (do this) and a decree (this is . . .). Luther takes both seriously.

> Here I beg each one who reads this little book to believe most firmly that these four men were not drunk or mad when they were writing and speaking these words; but, filled with the Holy Spirit, they wrote the truth of the matter, so that everyone may believe these words surely without wavering . . . .[39]

Continually searching for the greatest certainty as was possible, Luther finally relied on the gospel as the testimonial of the truth. These are the words of Christ, and these are the words to which our faith can cling.

Luther uses the Latin, *hic/hoc*,[40] when referring to the words of institution, which translate as "this, this here, this present moment, in this place." The term carries with it the force with which he believed in the Real Presence of Christ. It is located here in this bread, at this moment in this blood, here in this place for all to participate. It indicates specificity with regard to its object: it is *this* and not that; it is *here* and it is *now*. This bread is the body; This wine is the blood. It is no more complicated than that for him.

---

[38] Ibid., 53.
[39] Luther, "The Misuse of the Mass," (1521) in *LW* 36:163.
[40] "The Babylonian Captivity," 35.

In defense against those who, when discerning the meaning of "Real Presence," interpret scripture against Luther that "the flesh is of no avail," that mere flesh cannot ultimately benefit anyone, Luther relies again on the relationship between the finite and the infinite presence of God. Basically, Luther's counter to their challenge is that good works on their own merit are of no avail, and Jesus' flesh as mere flesh is of no avail, but each paired with the word of God and faith to receive the promise avail the believer of God's riches. Mere flesh and mere works gain a person nothing in the sight of God. But in the context of the promises of God, and accompanied by the word of God, the flesh of Christ and the works of the person can indeed become valuable vehicles for the divine. The sign must be accompanied by the significance and the faith.

What is at stake here is a key element in the theology of the eucharist for Luther: the Real Presence of Jesus' body and blood in the elements of bread and wine. He says that Jesus gave his true natural flesh (*sein wahrhaftig naturlich fleisch*) in the bread, and his natural true blood (*sein naturlich wahrhaftig blut*) in the wine, so that he would give a more complete sacrament or sign (*ein vollkommen sacrament oder zeichen gebe*)[41] It is important that the believer know that this is the true and natural (*wahrhaftig naturlich*) body and blood of Christ. In order to discern the meaning of this, human beings are counseled to put their energies into the faith that believes in the word of God. Because Christ says these words, says Luther, we must believe. "One must close mouth, eyes, and all the senses and say: 'Lord, you know better than I.'"[42] Reason and sensation based on outward experience serve us little when it comes to the sacraments and the faith which clings to the word of God. If we were to rely on these things at all, we would tread too close to relying on works instead of the word, which Christ counsels the individual to do.

We may understand that there is an incarnation of sorts which occurs in the sacrament to make these things present. Luther connects the Real Presence of the body and blood of Christ in the bread and wine of the sacrament to the incarnation of the Son of God in the womb of a virgin and to the presence of the two natures, divine and human, in the person of Jesus. Likewise, he uses an image that many refer to when trying to grasp what this means: "In red-hot iron, for instance, the two substances, fire and iron, are so mingled that every part is both iron and fire."[43] Our introduction to the

---

[41] German text from "*Ein Sermon von dem Hochwirdigen Sacrament des Heiligen Waren Leichnams Christi und von den Bruderschaften*," (1519) *Martin Luthers Werke: Kritische Gesammtausgabe* (Weimar: Bohlau, 1884) 2:749.

[42] Luther, "The Sacrament of the Body and Blood of Christ—Against the Fanatics,"(1526) in *LW* 36:345.

[43] "The Babylonian Captivity," 32.

axiom *finitum capax infiniti* has bearing here as well. Since we have affirmed that the divinity can be born of and within humanity and that God's word can infuse the finite elements of the sacrament, we can affirm that the body and blood of Christ are present in the bread and wine of the eucharist. "If God and man are one person and the two natures are so united that they belong together more intimately than body and soul, then Christ must also be man wherever he is God."[44] Luther's understanding of the Real Presence of Christ in the elements of the sacrament of eucharist is here closely tied to his understanding of the incarnation and two natures, divine and human, being really present in the person of Jesus Christ.

As for human experience of the sacrament, those senses which seem to contradict the contention for flesh and blood being present in the elements, Luther distinguishes between spiritual and physical in terms of sensation in eating (*leiblich und geistlich essen*):

> As far as taste is concerned the mouth surely seems to be eating something other than Christ's body. But the heart grasps the words in faith and eats spiritually precisely the same body as the mouth eats physically, for the heart sees very well what the uncomprehending mouth eats physically.[45]

The Real Presence of Christ in the sacrament is tied to the christological notions in Luther's theology, which again demonstrate God's commitment to humanity in the incarnation of Christ.

Luther, in his detailed exposition of the presence of Christ in the elements, affirms that Christ is not only in the physical bread and wine that human mouths taste, but continues to be present in other places and present with God.

> This does not mean that he is not present in other places also with his body and blood, for in believing hearts he is completely present with his body and blood. But it means that he wishes to make us certain as to where and how we are to lay hold of him.[46]

The finite, physical elements hold the body and blood of Christ, yet the infinite nature of God remains. If the (finite) human being [like Jesus] can hold the (infinite) presence of God [as Christ], then she is not only transformed, she embodies and is capable of expressing the vision of God. Luther's discussion of the three modes of presence should be recalled here.

---

[44] "Confession Concerning Christ's Supper," 231.
[45] Luther, "That These Word of Christ, 'This is My Body,' etc., Still Stand Firm Against the Fanatics," (1527) in *LW* 37:93.
[46] "The Sacrament of the Body and Blood of Christ—Against the Fanatics," 346.

> The first is this article of our faith, that Jesus Christ is essential, natural, true, complete God and man in one person, undivided and inseparable. The second, that the right hand of God is everywhere. The third, that the Word of God is not false or deceitful. The fourth, that God has and knows various ways to be present at a certain place, not only the single one of which the fanatics prattle, which the philosophers call "local."[47]

Luther's commitment to embodiment and human experience of the sacraments as well as to the mystery and power of God demonstrates a theological insistence on understanding human experience and its connection to God.

Through the last supper of Jesus and the implementation of the sacrament of the eucharist, two key phrases arise which Luther discusses in the Latin: *hoc est*, this is (my body, my blood), and *hoc facite*, do this (in remembrance of me.) Not only do we have the body and blood of Christ present, but we have been commanded to participate in them by the very word of the incarnate God. Christ's body, as broken for us in the past and in our presence, and Christ's blood, shed for the forgiveness of sins, are the means by which God encounters human beings at the table. The importance of embodiment and physical connection remains in our activity coming to the table and participating in the meal.

A question to be raised at this point, which will be addressed in the final chapter of this book, is this: When we hear *hoc facite*, and we respond, what is it that we are doing? The words of institution are clear that *hoc est* the body and blood, but what does that mean today, and what is the remembrance we are affirming when we do this? What is the active human response to the command, theologically speaking?

Luther understands the reality of sacrifice in this theology. "Christ's sacrifice is a living sacrifice, his body being sacrificed once on the cross and our bodies being sacrificed daily, a living holy sacrifice, which is a rational service of God. [Rom. 12:1]."[48] He is concerned in this statement to counter the Roman Catholic attempt to make the mass into a sacrifice, a work done by the priest that earns merit in the eyes of God. Luther upholds the notion that Jesus as Christ was sacrificed once in his death on the cross to atone for the sin of humanity. All work that needs to be done in order to restore humanity to relationship with God has been done in Jesus Christ, on the cross. There is nothing left for the human being to do. She can only believe: And even this is no work in the sight of God, for faith can never be a work. Luther recognizes the nature of the world to be such that "sacrifices" continue to occur, despite

---

[47] "Confession Concerning Christ's Supper," 214.

[48] "The Misuse of the Mass," 201.

the ultimate sacrifice which has been already made. In response, Christians are implored to go to the sacrament of *communio* in order to seek strength within the fellowship of saints and to remember the promises of God made in baptism.

For Luther, the sacrament of the eucharist is the one on which he spent much time and energy, in large part because he came under sharp criticism for his interpretation of it. We can see quite dramatically through his writing his understanding of the relationship between the human being and God, and between the human being and the world. The individual lives in a world which is less than ideal, a world which constantly challenges her faith and her sanctity in the presence of God. But it is critical for Luther that God allies with the human being through the sacrament of baptism initially and through the sacrament of the eucharist continually. He counsels that the eucharist ought to be celebrated "frequently." Daily life is a struggle and requires continual sustenance. The meal to which Christians come in public community is fuel for the soul and the body. The significance of the elements lies in part in their role as nourishment for the physical body and it also lies in the promise of God which they call us to remember. The faith with which they are received make them fully beneficial to the life of the individual who participates in community. It is important both that the believer go to the sacrament in *communio*, and that she understand that it was given for her. Both serve as strength for the journey that is human life *coram Deo*.

> Moreover, Eucharist meets that need, not by eating, but by sharing food, an act which demands the presence of an other and creates an interdependence between people. Each gives, each receives, and in this mutual reciprocity we are invited into a larger project: the work of the kingdom.[49]

A good friend of mine was a pastor in a small town in northwest Wisconsin. When she went for her initial interview with the call committee, she came back with only one concern about the church: the way in which they did communion. It was of some amusement that the practical elements of the call (the needs of the congregation, the personality of the senior pastor, the daily details of the job, even the location of the town) seemed to all be in place, but the one thing that gave her pause about this congregation was their communion practice—it was nothing like she had ever seen before!

In front of the pews, there are two movable communion rails—one on each side of the sanctuary. There is the typical kneeling rail and serving rail. But what is unique about this setup is that the tops of the serving rails flip

---

[49] Martha Ellen Stortz, "'Practicing what it means': Welfare Reform and the Lord's Supper," *CTM* 26 (February 1999) 32.

open to reveal a series of circular indentations and flat spaces. The circular spots are where the individual serving glasses of wine are placed (before the service) and the flat spaces are where trays of wafers are placed (before the service).

The process of communion is as follows: the ushers direct parishioners toward the front, where they kneel *en masse*. The presiding minister speaks the words of institution: "This is the body of Christ, broken for you." Each person in the entire assembled group then takes a wafer and eats it. The words are again spoken: "This is the blood of Christ, shed for you." The entire assembled group then takes a glass and drinks the wine. The promise is then spoken: "May the body and blood of our Lord Jesus Christ strengthen and preserve you . . . ." Then, the group is dismissed, and the next group comes forward and kneels, for the ritual to occur over and over until the entire community has participated.

We joked that this feels somewhat like "bellying up to God's bar." Irreverently so, it feels as if the group has bellied up to some bar and is doing shots. But I believe that this ritual lays bare some interesting things about the sacrament that I have not seen so clearly challenged anywhere else. These things became clear when my friend told me what happened when the sanctuary was being renovated, and the communion rails were not "flip-top" for a period of time. Communion was then distributed in a different manner: The group kneels, and the communion servers approach each person individually, and speak the words "This is the body of Christ, broken *for you*; This is the blood of Christ shed *for you*" to each person, and physically hand each person the wafer and the wine.

My friend said that something interesting occurred: She could tell that for some of the people, this was the only time that week that anyone had actually touched them, looked into their eyes, and said that anything was for them. This powerfully shows us what impact the words and the sacrament can and perhaps ought to have for Christians. This is not just some rote thing that we do out of memory and tradition. This is a dramatic moment, in which the pastor is speaking the word of God to each individual who has come to participate in *communio*. This is *for you*. Jesus did this, God did this, this was done, *for you*.

Luther held up the importance of faith, of understanding and accepting that the work of God in Christ is *pro me*. It is also important that the sacrament take place publicly, and that it convey in some way the presence of God in community. We can see in this illustration how that can be expressed and how that can draw out important elements of the community. There is a tension of sorts between the individual and the communal levels of the significance of the eucharist, one that is manifest in this illustration. The "regular" way in which the community participates in the sacrament symbolizes the communal/meal-at-table aspect of the eucharist, while the "individual" distribution method symbolizes another true meaning of the sacrament—that it is *for you*. The "flip-top" communion rails came back to my friend's church, and the community there was challenged, at least for a short time, to discern what is actually happening and what is being expressed in this sacrament.

Criticism and Appreciation: Response and Interpretation with Contemporary Theology

In this section of the chapter, I wish to undertake two main tasks: First, to revisit and evaluate some of the principles and assertions of Luther's sacramental theology from the perspectives of the contemporary theological schools explored in chapter two. This will enable us to both discern points of theological congruity and divergence between them. Each may show advantage and challenge to the other. Second, I want to invite some other partners into the theological discussion—namely some contemporary Luther scholars and some feminist theologians working specifically with sacramental theology. They will serve to both enrich the project and focus the issues a bit more sharply. What is at issue with each of these schools of thought? What resources will we take from this collection of theologians to move into addressing critical contemporary issues regarding the relationship between God and the human being?

"Feminist" and Process Theologies Encounter Luther

Reading Luther from the perspective of the contemporary theological proposals presented in chapter two raises some interesting issues. The intention of bringing them together is not to validate or justify one or the other but to see how each raises questions of the other. Both take with utmost seriousness the relationship between the human being and God, and particular theological understandings of these characters play into their theologies. As a general observation that will guide the course of this exploration, I will state my assessment of the issues: Luther serves this project well and helps contemporary theologians in discerning the nature and dynamics of the relationship between God and the human being, but fails us in presenting appropriate understandings of the human *qua* human, and God *qua* God through his sacramental theology. Luther pushes us toward centering theology on the work and gifts of God, and contemporary theologies insist on accounting for the concrete reality of human life in any conversation. Bringing the two together illumines this tension and allows for the gifts of each to challenge and enrich the other.

Let us consider the concrete reality of human life. Human nature in its fleshly state of affairs, for Luther, is wretched, sinful, corrupt on its own. Luther states that the human being, by virtue of being born of the flesh, is born in sin and needs to die to the "old" life and be born anew in life with Christ. One must be reborn with the word of the Father in order to receive the riches of Christ. His images of immersion in baptism suggest very specifically the cycle of death and rebirth that is critical to his theology. In this, Luther insists that the person be brought low, be made humble, be drowned to an old life and to find new, cleansed, spiritual rebirth and life in Christ and in the community of saints. We can see where the problems come in, in conversation with feminist theologians. The need for death or humiliation of the inadequate person in order to attain blessing and gift from God immerses the notion of being human in being brought low, dying to an old self, and being reborn in a blessed life through the power of the Father.

Luther's presentation of the human being in relationship with God can indeed serve us well, however, as the human being is valued as a child of God, as a creation of God, and as an ally with God. God's commitment to the human being is unwavering and intimate, and is unrivaled throughout human life. This simultaneous criticism and retrieval of Luther's presentation of the human being is due in part to the fact that Luther finds it hard to think of the human being outside of the relationship with God. His approach to theological anthropology (if we may impose a category on him) is decidedly more theo-centric than our present project, which may tend toward the anthropocentric.

The human being according to Luther is so enmeshed in evil and suffering that she can do little of her own volition but despair. The struggles of human life cannot be effectively dealt with by the individual alone, for Luther. It is only with the help of God that she can have strength enough to ultimately overcome evil and temptation. While many debate Luther's ethics and social reform, and some argue that he presented effective means with which social reform could come about, we will focus here on the theological implications of what we have seen in his sacramental theology.[50]

I wish to frame the issue of life in the world in part between *Anfechtung* and *la lucha*. We have seen from two different sources how "struggle" is characteristic of human life in the world. For Luther, this was cause to seek God and take comfort in one's baptism. The suffering and trials of human life serve a purpose in this manner of thinking—to drive the individual back to

---

[50] The previously cited article [Stortz, "'Practicing what it means'"] presents a compelling case for understanding Luther's priesthood of all believers and the eucharist as models for welfare civics and social reform. See also George W. Forell, *Faith Active In Love: An Investigation of the Principles Underlying Luther's Social Ethics* (New York: American, 1954).

her baptism and back to her dependence on God. Together God and the human being set out to slay sin. *Anfechtung* can be understood as an open and personal struggle, a psycho-spiritual tension that fills the human being with uncertainty and tentativity (from *tentatio*). Definitions of the German term include contestation and temptation. For Isasi-Díaz, *la lucha* is first understood to be a characteristic of human life, and then it is used as occasion to define and call for human agency. She contrasts suffering with the struggle and shows how the struggle is a location for human life. This allows us to understand human agency as working within and out of that in order to bring about, as she calls it, a preferred future. Isasi-Díaz's use of *la lucha* emphasizes the social struggle, the public work for justice in the community.

In speaking of both *Anfechtung* and *la lucha*, God's presence with the person helps to alleviate pain and strengthen the individual. Luther's use of the term *Anfechtung* calls forth the sense of being publicly tempted or challenged. It reflects the struggle which was Luther's personal struggle: to be accepted before God. *La lucha* is framed in such a way that it is an inevitable part of the fabric of life for women in the world. It reflects the social and cultural status of Hispanic women for Isasi-Díaz. The point for Luther is that the person ultimately relies on the relationship with God to find strength in the suffering, and that the understanding that God is with us alleviates the anxiety. The point for Isasi-Díaz is that the person work outward from the underlying presence of God to effect change in the world. Both theologians rely on the relationship with God for strength, while perhaps reflecting the larger themes of their theology when detailing human struggle and action in the world.

It is the relationship between God and the human being that comes from Luther as human life *coram Deo* which expresses the relationship which is also central for feminist and process theologians. Process theologians emphasize with great detail the presence of God in the world, in the details of creation, and in the continuous process of human life. They do this using philosophical resources, while we find again and again in Luther an unwillingness to define the human being outside of the notion of being *coram Deo*. Likewise, in the principles from womanist theology that we explored in Karen Baker-Fletcher's proposal, God is the Creator who gifts all of creation with a spark of divinity, and to be human means to live with this gift and its responsibility. This illustrates a deeper sense of human responsibility in the contemporary context of the relationship with God, where the human being can even be spoken of as a created co-creator, working with God. Whether it be the way in which Whitehead understands God as continually presenting initial aims luring the world toward fulfillment, but never determining the decisions of the world, or the way in which Baker-Fletcher speaks of humanity's responsibility to exercise gifts of vision and sustenance with God, these theologians emphasize and affirm human agency within the relationship in a way that Luther did not. This discussion of human agency affirms the need for grasping the responsibility and capability that goes along with being human in the world.

Throughout this discussion, we see a difference of approach between Luther and contemporary theologians. Luther's thoroughly theo-centric approach affects how he presents the relationship between God and the human being in his sacramental theology. God acts, God moves, God gives, and God promises. Process and feminist theologians, as we have examined them in this book, have a keen interest in preserving the agency of humanity when speaking about the relationship between God and the world. This interest reflects a form of optimism that we can do something, but it involves an intense realism that accounts for the sufferings of the world throughout human history. The sense is not of despair and tragedy, rather it allows for a theological approach which engages human being working in the world for the purposes of God. Reclaiming the value of these things is done not to take value and power away from God, but to attempt to strengthen an understanding about the relationship between God and the world.

These distinctions between the dynamics of relationship, and the characters of God and the human being, make further sense when we consider Luther's context as it demanded different things from his theology. Perhaps the urgency with which contemporary theologians feel the crises of ecological demise, cultural battle lines, economic doom, or secularized cultures demands that they view human life in the world in a much different manner. The crises faced by Luther were different and demanded different attentions. The fact that the present crises demand immediate and detailed attention in order to preserve large-scale global well-being forces the theologian to reckon with what is being said about human life in the world and in relationship with God. In order to preserve life, we must be able to do something. Neither human action or God's power can be ignored, and each should be explicated in terms of the other. This is what we mean when we seek to understand human life *coram Deo*. It is first of all a *human* life, but it is always *coram Deo*.

The relationship between the human being and God explicated by Marjorie Suchocki in her discussion of sin helps us to understand how God and the human being relate. God becomes an underlying and secondary (albeit inescapable) aspect of the human being's life in the world. Because it is tremendously important to address the effects of human activity (including sin) in the world and because we presume God's presence in the world, our activity either in violation or in preservation of well-being is *therefore* in relationship to and affecting God. The balance between these two avenues of relationship is precarious and precious. Humanity lives simultaneously *coram mundo* and *coram Deo*: Luther helps contemporary theologies to grasp to power of the latter, while they attend more to the former and its consequences. Both approaches must come together in order to account for the fullness of life.

God possesses all power for Luther: the power of grace, of forgiveness, and of love. Only through the encounter with this divine perfection of power can the human hope to attain any sense of goodness. With God, the human being has a chance to effect transformation in the world, working as she will in accord with the vision of God. The connections between these ways of understanding the human being's relationship with God is nuanced, but it depends on the way in which the human being herself is understood. For Luther, the individual, while fulfilling his or her own *vocatio* (call or role in life) in the community, is faltering and struggling daily to slay sin. For our contemporary conversation partners, the individual works out of her context, within the world, for the purpose of transformation and the vision of God. The former depends on an understanding of God as in control, fully powerful and wise in regard to the fate of the world. The latter depends on some understanding of the power of God as mutually related to the power of the world. We saw a clear presentation of that out of Whitehead's cosmology and Johnson's development of God as Sophia.

The alliance between God and the human being in Luther's sacramental theology is to be celebrated and used as a resource for our present theological construction. His emphasis on the overwhelming presence and power of God pushes our contemporary theological sources to take the divine seriously. And while this relational emphasis is effective, his attempt to affirm that human beings do have a responsibility to act in the temporal world in such a manner as to embody the love of God or be "little Christs" to one another, however, does little to affirm anything essentially good about the human *being on her own*. This distinction matters.

It is important to finally note the powerfully constructive aspects of Luther's sacramental theology: the presence of God in and to human struggle demonstrates God's deep commitment to be with humanity and the world. It also affirms God's vulnerability which is a result of this commitment to the world. The embodiment of this commitment in the sacraments provides a physical means through which human beings can express their faith in and experience of God's presence throughout their lives. The relationship between God and the human being is one which is very intimate—in fact it seems inescapable. God is present at birth, eating, death, suffering and celebration in human life. It is these dynamics of deep relationality which will serve the proposal in its final moments.

Feminist Roman Catholic Scholarship and Finnish Luther Scholarship

I now end this chapter with a brief exploration of other "options" for discussing the sacraments and their expression of the relationship between God and the human being within contemporary theology. One comes from Luther scholars working in Finland, and the other comes from Roman Catholic feminist theologians who directly address sacramental theology. Each picks up on some of the issues that we have highlighted in this chapter, and gives a new spin to the questions.

Two Feminist Roman Catholic Scholars

Christine Gudorf argues that the sacraments of the Christian church are appreciative expressions of the life process itself which Jesus affirmed in his life and teaching. As a Roman Catholic theologian, she deals with the seven sacraments of her tradition. She argues that most of them, including baptism and eucharist, with which we are concerned here, are ritualized forms of the things that women do as part of natural life-giving processes: birth, feeding, rites of passage, comforting and so on. The intention of her analysis is as follows:

> If we are to save the power and meaning of sacraments, whose purpose is to induce appreciation of and commitment to God's gift of created life, we must not only move toward recognizing the ritual powers of women, but also, and probably first, address the exclusion of males from the activities sacraments model. Only then can sacraments cease to be weapons in a war between the sexes.[51]

We see how her concern is not only to ordain women into the leadership of the church but to encourage the participation of men in the social and nurturing activities that the sacraments imitate. She stops short of a blatant charge that the church co-opts women's experience by taking the things that they can do naturally and raising them up to an acceptable spiritualized plane. This can be derived from her analysis, however. The larger issue is the gender imbalance when it comes to both the social and the sacramental.

Gudorf's assessment of the sacraments and their connection to natural processes of giving life, feeding, nurturing and sustaining presents a clear concern for God's affirmation of and participation in human life and its embodiedness. She seeks not to rail against the church for its denigration of women's experience and its need to give men a means by which to do the

---

[51] Christine Gudorf, "The Power to Create: Sacraments and Men's Need to Birth," *Horizons* 14 (1987) 309.

things that women do naturally, rather she wants to make the implicit connections between the social and the spiritual explicit. In doing so, we are enabled to further see how the sacraments affirm the physicality of the world, and the embodiedness of human life. "The sacraments should not draw our attention away from 'ordinary' human life, but should transform 'ordinary' life by causing us to understand it more deeply."[52] To view the sacraments as a celebration with God for the processes of life leads us to an affirmation of those very processes. This is perhaps one way in which we can see the need to affirm the value of the finite (physical) in and of itself.

Susan Ross develops four criteria for a feminist sacramental theology that further assist us in focusing these issues. First, she calls for "tolerance and appreciation for ambiguity."[53] By this, she means to avoid the dualistic tendencies of valid or invalid expressions of the sacraments, real or symbolic versions of God's presence, and the boundaries between clergy and lay persons in the community. We can see how this could help us approach Luther—what if we affirm the real presence of Christ, but faithfully maintain some sense of the ambiguity of this statement? We don't ultimately know what is happening in the sacrament, and perhaps we don't need to. We can take the theological importance of such an affirmation as part of his incarnational theology, and retain a sense of ambiguity and mystery about what this actually means in terms of an experience of the sacrament.

The second suggestion is for "a critical consideration of theories of body and gender."[54] It is in this realm where we are enabled to ask the questions of what it means for Luther to insist that we are drowned and raised in new life, what it means that we participate in the death of Christ through the sacrament of the eucharist. How does taking women's experience seriously change the questions and the issues surrounding sacramental theology? In considering the body when we speak about the sacraments, we consider human experience in all of its particularities. We also are driven to affirm the value of the body in itself.

The third criterion Ross proposes is that sacramental theology "include a critical understanding of theories of symbolic representation."[55] This is not to move toward understanding a symbolic presence in the eucharist, but to look at the sacraments and their theological significance, to see here what they symbolically represent with regard to the human being and her relation-

---

[52] Ibid., 305.

[53] Susan A. Ross, *Extravagant Affections: A Feminist Sacramental Theology* (New York: Continuum, 1998) 54.

[54] Ibid., 57.

[55] Ibid., 59.

ship with God. Notions of dependence and humiliation may have unique difficulty when approached from the vantage point of women's experiences of the world. To suggest that a person happily bear profitable suffering so that it drives her closer to God carries implications beyond the theological in our contemporary social realm where many peoples, particularly women, are asked to suffer for the greater good, to put their needs and desires aside for the benefit of the others.

Finally, Ross suggests that "an adequate sacramental theology is ultimately judged by its struggle to overcome oppression and work for justice."[56] For Roman Catholic women such as Gudorf and Ross, the justice issue necessarily includes the question of women's ordination. For others, the affirmation of God's presence in the world and God's alliance with the human being must say something about what it means to be a human, *being* and *doing* in the world. The relationship ought to serve to enhance human efforts for justice and transformation in the world. God's power in the world ought to be understood as a radical presence of grace and a creative lure toward emancipation. If only one of the points of sacramental theology is to express the presence of God in the physical world, then that theology ought to enable human beings to make a difference in that world according to the vision of God. This asks and suggests an answer to the question: What difference does the presence of God make?

Finnish Scholarship

We now conclude with insights on the union of God and the human being from the school of contemporary Finnish Luther scholars. Simo Peura presents an argument which seeks to understand the Real Presence of Christ through the notion of deification. His position depends on affirming an ontological justification. Basically, deification (*theosis, Vergöttlichung*, the process by which human nature is transformed in deep ontological union with God) comes about in the believer through faith, and is realized when Christ inhabits the believer. The point of this is to affirm that the unification of Christ with the human being allows the person to participate in the saving properties of Christ, the gifts of God. There is a definite sense of the mystical about this presentation of the deification of the human being as justification and ontological renewal. The Real Presence of Christ is what makes human participation in God and God's nature possible.[57]

---

[56] Ibid., 62.
[57] The sustained argument is to be found in Simo Peura, *Mehr als ein Mensch? Die Vergöttlichung as Thema der Theologie Martin Luthers von 1513–1519*, Veröffentlichungen des Instituts für Europäische Geschichte Mainz 152 (Mainz: von Zaubern, 1994).

Peura also addresses baptism as the moment wherein God unites with the believer: "through the sacramental act of baptism, God binds himself ontologically to a sinner and is one with him through his whole earthly life, if he adheres to Christ in faith."[58] He speaks of baptism as the way in which God initiates faith in the human being, and joins with the person and empowers her to struggle against sin. The continuing presence of sin in the world requires the human being to be gifted with the real presence of Christ and a union with God for strength and sustenance. This presumes what Tuomo Mannermaa explicates as Christ as *maxima persona*, the supreme person, "in whom the persons of all human beings are united in a real manner."[59] We must understand that *unio cum Christo*, as Peura suggests it, depends on the notion that within the person of Christ the conquest of sin and evil took place, and that we are to understand him as the greatest person, in whom all believers are united and can share in the victory over sin and evil.

The brief introduction to this line of interpreting Luther's theology cannot do justice to its provocations, particularly its turn toward the mystical elements, but it does highlight the questions we have pertaining to Luther. We see here an even deeper understanding of the dynamic relationship between God and the human being. Peura proposes an ontological unification as the most effective way to understand the presence of Christ and the unity between God and the human being. Christ and the human being participate in each other in a deeply intimate manner—each sharing in the burdens and the riches of the other. However, we are left with the sense of inadequacy in human nature *per se*. For it is the relationship with God, the life *coram Deo*, that fundamentally guides Luther's understanding of humanity.

Concluding Remarks

Luther's writings on the sacraments present in vivid and dramatic form his understanding of the relationship between God and the human being. In doing so, he tells us much about what he believes about human nature in itself and the character of God in itself. The depth with which he probes the relationship between God and the human being is the greatest gift of his theology for this book. The centeredness of God in Luther's theology challenges the tendency of contemporary feminist and process theologians to center the human issues. The unfailing covenant between God and the human being,

---

[58] Peura, "Christ as Favor and Gift (*donum*): The Challenge of Luther's Understanding of Justification," in *Union with Christ: The New Finnish Interpretation of Luther*, ed. Carl E. Braaten and Robert W. Jenson (Grand Rapids: Eerdmans, 1998) 54.

[59] Tuomo Mannermaa, "Justification and Theosis in Lutheran-Orthodox Perspective," in Braaten and Jenson, *Union with Christ*, 30.

which Luther presents along with the incarnation experienced and fulfilled in the person of Jesus as Christ, is nothing short of a marvel. It fulfills a need to understand the commitment of God to the world, and helps us to understand the commitment of the world to the vision of God.

However, as we have seen, Luther does not fill our present need to understand what it means to be a human being, and what it means for God to be God in relationship to that. Thus, we have turned back to contemporary theology in feminism and process thought to weave in resources that address the concerns for emancipation and transformation. We also see hints of what this conversation may mean for Christology and atonement. If we take from chapter one the need for theology to move beyond speaking of human subjectivity to addressing human agency and the contemporary resources from chapter two that address this very question, we can approach a traditional theology of the sacraments seeing that some work needs to be done regarding the relationship between God and the human being.

At the outset of this chapter, I stated that Luther would serve to both challenge and inspire our present work. The challenge lies in the theocentric way in which he understands the relationship of God to the world. For reasons that pertain to his own context and personal struggles, Luther preserved and explicated the power and graciousness of God. The inspiration lies in the detailed and careful manner in which he presents the dynamic of relationality between God and the world. God is a concerned and committed character in this relationship, and the human being gains immensely and eternally from being in the relationship. The challenge remains in the limitations of Luther's understanding of being human, which was tied to his 16th century social and theological context. Certain aspects of the theological conversation about the human being transcend time: the way we understand the individual and the role of faith and life in the church, the way we see God working throughout human life, and the way trust is ultimately placed in God. However, in the twenty-first century, we must be equipped to address the particular needs and concerns of the human community. This is where we must diverge from Luther.

Through a reinterpretation of Luther, we can discern an adequate alternative for the present in a theological proposal that uses important aspects of his thought, while bringing them to light in a theological and political context that is very different from their origin. This helps us to address the relationship between God and the human being as it has implications for Christology and atonement. What does it mean to hold up human agency and divine mutuality from contemporary theologies with a covenantal relationship and a powerfully gracious God from Luther's sacramental theology, when looking at the events of the life, death, and resurrection of Jesus as

Christ? It is there that we discover the impetus of the sacraments and a core expression of the relationship between God and the human being.

4

The Mission of Jesus and the Vision of God:
Implications for Christology and Atonement

In the introduction to this book I stated that a commitment to feminist theological criticism of christology[1] and particularly atonement theory grounds what I identify to be a problem of theology, particularly as it pertains to the relationship between God and the human being which is concretely manifest in the sacraments. The problem lies in the connection of the suffering and death of Jesus with the redemption of the human race, and the way in which the sacrament of the eucharist celebrates and lifts up these events as definitive for the relationship between God and the human being. It is the task of this chapter to return to those problems by exploring some traditions of atonement theory, examining the feminist criticism of it, and then seeing the ways in which a reconstructed understanding of the relationship between God and the human being as we have been developing can address some of the critical issues. The work of the previous chapters on illumining the way in which we speak about the relationship between God and the human being leads us back to the problems stated at the outset, and provides a means with which we can suggest answers to the questions. This chapter will explore atonement in light of the theological proposals offered in chapters one and two, and will tie in with the work of Luther on the sacraments presented in chapter three in order to suggest a final proposal for sacramental theology in the following chapter.

As was stated at the outset of this project, the problem lies in the contention that the death of Jesus on the cross, necessary or not, *is* the means

---

[1] I am using the term "christology" in a somewhat loose manner, to indicate general conversation about the person of Jesus and interpretations of his life, death, and significance.

by which human beings have been restored to right relationship with God. The need for death in order to bring about life is questioned most deeply throughout this study: We saw how Luther's sacramental theology set up the cycle of death and rebirth, and it was suggested that this is not an adequate way in which to understand human life. With suffering and death definitively in the symbolic center of Christian theology, particularly as the means of relational restoration on the cross, we are forced to confront the reality of suffering, abuse, death, and evil in the world. Confronting this in context of the relationship between God and the human being determines the way we speak about God's presence and human responsibility in the world. This is a point of departure for theological reflection, and has often been a point of departure for destructive assumptions and violent practices. The guiding questions for discussing Christology and atonement theory include: Where is God? Who is the human being? What is God's role? Why did Jesus die? And, Why did Jesus live?

Having moved through the previous steps of this study, we can propose answers to several of these questions—hopefully in a provocative way. The previous chapters have attempted to address the relationship between God and the human being and the questions about who each of these characters is, and our subsequent reflection on the questions about Jesus will lead us to propose a renewed understanding of a theology of the eucharist. This attempt to shift the way in which we understand the human being, the character of God, and the relationship between the two is the key to this present exploration of christology and atonement theory. We have seen hints throughout this project of what some contemporary proposals and our traditional resource identified in Luther may say about Jesus as Christ, as the one through whom humanity is brought into right relation with God. This demonstrates how intimately bound these notions are within any systematic theology.

This chapter will first briefly examine two traditional Christian thinkers who inform much of what has been said about christology and atonement. This will serve to frame the criticism that grounds the presuppositions and commitments of this project. We will then attend to the specific charges identified in the phrase "divine child abuse," within feminist theology. Some of the theological proposals already examined in this project will return as they offer response and creative means by which we can think about Jesus as Christ, and the events of his life, death, and resurrection. Finally, we will attempt to reframe the issues by addressing the questions of God's presence and the reasons for Jesus' death as they are aided by our analysis of the relationship between God and the human being. The ways in which we approach and answer these questions will set the stage for our final return to sacramental theology as it is a prime manifestation of the relationship between God and the human being and a particular consequence of the story of Jesus.

Atonement Theories: Traditional Voices

Atonement theories maintain, in some form or another, that Jesus' death restores humanity to right relationship with God. "Atonement ('at-onement,' a sixteenth-century coinage) is the reconciliation of sinners with God, especially through the cross, as communicated through the gospel and the sacraments."[2] For purposes of this project, we are analyzing atonement primarily in terms of its reflection of the relationship between God and the human being.[3] Atonement is based on the assertion that God and humanity *were* reconciled through the suffering and death of Jesus on the cross. Implications of this are the concern of the present chapter, and we will see the differing ways in which it is responded to by select theologians. It is important to note that within Christian thinking, atonement as this reconciliation is communicated through the sacraments. Both atonement theory and sacramental theology are affected by what we assert about the relationship between God and the human being.

Various "types" of atonement theories exist within Christian tradition. Themes include sacrifice, propitiation, substitution, reconciliation, and ransom. It is beyond the scope of this project to examine traditional atonement theory in its depth and breadth, but I do wish to illumine a few thematic points and definitions to contextualize the criticism and the subsequent proposal. Because of my theological context, I focus on the dominant Western type of atonement theory growing out of Anselm because I believe that the questions and the challenges we are faced with in contemporary theology stem in part from the themes in his thought. These are themes that cut across many theologians' work on the atonement and they are being questioned here. These themes develop the basic assertion of atonement theory noted above – that we must reflect on suffering and death as the means by which humanity was put in right relationship with God. This is problematic in that it allows Christian theology to presuppose suffering and death as the center of discussion about the relationship between God and the human being. This presupposition speaks volumes about God and the human being, and their relationship, and it plays forth in themes of various atonement theories.

---

[2] Eugene Teselle, "Atonement," in *A New Handbook of Christian Theology*, ed. Donald W. Musser and Joseph L. Price (Nashville: Abingdon, 1992) 41.

[3] Theories of atonement and centuries of detailed theological reflection upon it certainly go beyond the parameters of this project.

Definitions and Themes: From Anselm and Abelard

Two classic formulations of atonement theory are found within the writings of St. Anselm of Canterbury and Peter Abelard of the eleventh and twelfth centuries respectively. Each has influenced the Christian tradition of atonement theories. We find Anselm's line of thought more directly criticized in this project while Abelard presents a way of looking at the issues of atonement that begins the move in the direction this book hopes to go. For purposes of this chapter, we will focus on how each theologian presents and approaches the importance of the death of Jesus as means to restoring the relationship between God and the human being in some major writings.

Anselm says of the obedience of Jesus to the will of God in his *"Cur Deus Homo"*: "for he held out so firmly in this obedience that he met death on account of it. It may, indeed be said, that the Father commanded him to die, when he enjoined that upon him. . . ."[4] For Anselm, it is presumed first of all that only God possesses the power to redeem humanity, and asserted that the obedience of the incarnate one, divine/human Jesus Christ, becomes the means by which all of humanity is restored to God. This Son of God was perfectly obedient to the will of God:

> But he speaks of the will of the Father, not because the Father preferred the death of the Son to his life; but because the Father was not willing to rescue the human race, unless man were to do even as great a thing as was signified in the death of Christ. . . . [The Son] preferred to suffer, rather than that the human race should be lost;[5]

Coupled with the unwillingness of the Father to rescue humanity is the gift of the Son to suffer for the salvation of humanity. Anselm suggests that the Father did not prefer death to life, but that it was the only way.

Throughout Anselm's writing, the suffering and death of the Son is acknowledged and lifted up as that which was both willed by the Father and chosen by the Son in obedience. The Father wills it because He was not willing to rescue humanity without some intervention. The need for something to be done on behalf of the desolate human race is critical for Anselm. Humanity is caught up in the world and unable to bring itself to reconciliation with God. Anselm speaks also about the "debt" owed to God, the honor which is due Him and has been taken away from Him by sin. He calls this honor the "satisfaction which every sinner owes to God,"[6] and he speaks of

---

[4] *Basic Writings*, *"Cur Deus Homo,"* trans. S. W. Deane, 2d ed. (LaSalle, Ill.: Open Court, 1962) 194.

[5] Ibid., 196.

[6] Ibid., 203.

the need for satisfaction in order for there to be salvation. The death of Jesus was a necessity because God needed all of these things. Anselm's concept of God comes through strongly in these images.

The obedience of Jesus is also a crucial point for Anselm. He speaks of it in such a way that lifts obedience to the level of ultimate human virtue in response to God: "But he suffered death of his own will, not yielding up his life as an act of obedience, but on account of his obedience in maintaining holiness; for he held out so firmly in this obedience that he met death on account of it."[7] Anselm frames this in a way that makes obedience to holiness the virtue, not obedience to an order from God. Jesus' death is a result of his commitment to God, a result of his own will and a product of his obedience to a holy life. The conflagration of death and obedience is one of Anselm's most troubling legacies. "[H]e used those words, viz., to teach the human race that there was no other salvation for them but by his own death; and not to show that he had no power at all to avoid death."[8] The death of Jesus is the only way for humanity to be reconciled with God, and Jesus' obedience is the way in which this comes about. When speaking about the action of the incarnate Son, themes like obedience, satisfaction, debt and payment come out strongly in Anselm's theology, and they continue to impact Christian theology in the modern era.

Peter Abelard raises some of the same critical questions of Anselm's thought that we will raise in the latter portions of this chapter. Although he remains influenced by him, Abelard diverges from the path of Anselm. Here we see a shift in the way Jesus' death is presented:

> In what way does the apostle declare that we are justified or reconciled to God through the death of his Son, when God ought to have been the more angered against man, inasmuch as men acted more criminally by crucifying his Son than they ever did by transgressing his first command in paradise through the tasting of a single apple?[9]

His answers to his own question pertain to the Anselmian themes we have discussed and move in the direction of the proposals of this project. We see that Jesus' death is here mentioned as a result of the criminal actions of men, not solely as a result of a perfectly obedient Son. But Abelard also says that the teachings and example of Jesus are the means by which God binds Himself to humanity, and that the example of Jesus who teaches us even by his death,

---

[7] Ibid., 194.

[8] Ibid., 199.

[9] Peter Abelard, "Exposition of the Epistle to the Romans (An Excerpt from the Second Book)," in *A Scholastic Miscellany: Anselm to Ockham*, ed. and trans. Eugene Rathbone Fairweather (Philadelphia: Westminster, 1961) 282.

ought to move the human spirit to fuller and deeper expressions of love and thankfulness for the grace of God.

Abelard moves away from the strict necessitation of the death of Jesus for reconciliation between God and humanity, but he maintains its power and goodness through insisting that we recognize the depth of divine love and grace in Christ's death.

> Now it seems to us that we have been justified by the blood of Christ and reconciled to God in this way: through this unique act of grace manifested to us—in that his Son has taken upon himself our nature and persevered therein in teaching us by word and example even unto death—he has more fully bound us to himself by love; with the result that our hearts should be enkindled by such a gift of divine grace....[10]

The greatness of God is what Abelard emphasizes, "even unto death." He sees humanity redeemed through the death of Jesus, but he emphasizes that human redemption in Christ's suffering ought to bring forth hearts "enkindled." Where Anselm conflated obedience and death, Abelard associates love and spiritual conversion with death. However, he also speaks of those things which Jesus taught through his life, "by word and example." The shift that we see in Abelard is one that moves away from the penal satisfaction imagery of Anselm, and toward moral and spiritual imagery that is often more readily accepted in contemporary theological projects. This will be important to the proposals later in this chapter.

A danger of Abelard's presentation, however, remains in the way he associates love and spiritual conversion with the suffering and death of Jesus. His writing is full of language that refers to the moral examples and actions that Jesus undertook throughout his life. This emphasis on the life and teaching of Jesus is valuable, but Abelard brings it to consummation in the ultimate example of Jesus' death. This death is so powerful that it ought to move the hearts of human beings toward giving thanks for the grace of God which saves them. So while Abelard provides us with questions and answers that address some of our concerns, he remains within the tradition of explicating the power and greatness of Jesus' suffering and death on the cross.

Anselm's and Abelard's reflections on their theories of the atonement set a general, albeit limited, basis from which we can move into understanding contemporary theological response to and construction on the atonement. Anselm maintains the idea of an omnipotent, transcendent God who is not satisfied with the workings of the human world. Humanity is not sufficient, nor is it wholly pleasing. The failings of the human community and the de-

---

[10] Ibid., 283.

mands of the divine reality thread through his proposal and present the dynamic of relationship between God and the human being that we have come to question throughout the course of this project.

For Anselm, the human race would have been lost were it not for the suffering and death of the Son—this is the satisfaction that God required. The language includes "rescue" and "debt" and "desired the death of the Son." These themes unequivocally uphold the death of Jesus as the only way in which God could be satisfied, and in which humanity could be restored to God's grace. Humanity is unable to do anything, and God is unwilling to simply "rescue."

For Abelard, humanity is still justified by the blood of Christ. Jesus' death on the cross is the means of reconciliation, and it is the means which ought to move humanity toward spiritual conversion. The point here, however, is not the satisfaction of God through death, it is the example for life that Jesus provided to the world. This is the difference from Anselm that we must lift up out of Abelard. He focuses on the love of God for the world as demonstrated through the *life* of Jesus, even insisting that those who crucified him were criminal. The words and actions of Jesus are lifted up here as the way in which God is bound to humanity. The life of Jesus expresses God's commitment to the human community, and it is a critical part of our understanding the relationship between the two. His suggestion is that human beings ought to respond "with hearts enkindled," and in faith. Abelard begins the shift toward lifting up the importance of the life of Jesus, as opposed to the centrality of his death. This is the move that this project hopes to continue.

Aulén and the Atonement: Typology and Response

In 1930, Gustaf Aulén presented a historical, classic, and also historically questionable, scheme with which the atonement is often understood. Scholars have since suggested that his typology may be interesting, but that his historical interpretations of particular thinkers are faulty. Some take particular issue with Aulén, and we will introduce their criticisms here. Analytically, however, his typology has proven to be useful, and it, along with its criticism, serves to illumine some of the themes which we have presented in the foregoing and to provide entrée into the contemporary conversations about atonement.

Aulén formulates three types of atonement theory, each of which proposes a particular way to understand God and humanity. He draws several conclusions concerning the relationship between them from these three types.

> The classic type showed us the Atonement as a *movement of God to man*, as God as closely and personally engaged in the work of man's deliverance.
>
> . . .
>
> In the Latin type, God seems to stand more at a distance; for the satisfaction is paid by man, in the person of Christ, to God.
>
> . . .
>
> In the third type God stands still more at a distance; as far as He is concerned, no atonement is needed, and all the emphasis is on *man's movement to God*, on that which is accomplished in the world of men.[11]

These types of atonement theory variously emphasize the activity of God and of the human being. Aulén suggests that the classic type of atonement theory has been present throughout most of Christian history, and that its influence is considerable. It is here that we find the presentation of divine power as the impetus for all things related to restoring humanity to God. It is fully God's work and there is no way in which human beings deserve or can earn the grace of deliverance from sin. The classic type presents the notion of the Christus Victor—the victorious Christ—who is the agent of triumph over the forces of sin, death, and the devil.

In the Latin type, satisfaction is framed in legalistic terms: "Images and analogies are taken continually from the law-courts in the manner dear to the Latin mind."[12] The cycle of judgment/penalty/restitution dominates the Latin type. Aulén associates Anselm with this type, and acceptably so. We saw in our previous introduction to Anselm's *"Cur Deus Homo"* that God demands some form of satisfaction, a demonstration of honor, in order to restore righteousness to humanity. Humans have failed, and God demands that justice be done, a penalty be paid, and honor be restored.

The third type, which Aulén terms "the subjective," emphasizes the processes within humanity—the "conversion and amendment" of humanity in accord with the example of Jesus. Moral and ethical ideals come into play here, and human beings are the characters continually striving to become more like Jesus in order to be more appealing to God. Abelard is the chief representative of this type, Aulén suggests. Jesus is the example of humanity that we all ought to strive to be; He exemplifies the best that humanity can be when in proper relationship with the divine.

---

[11] Gustaf Aulén, *Christus Victor: An Historical Study of the Three Main Types of the Idea of the Atonement*, trans. A. G. Hebert (New York: Macmillan, 1931, 1951) 171.

[12] Ibid., 163.

For our purposes, Aulén's typology reaffirms some of the themes of atonement theory, and divides them in three sets of concepts, each addressing its own concerns through its own emphases. Most of these concepts still pervade our traditions, theologies, and confessions. The "classical" notion of God's freeing humanity from bondage to sin and evil is affirmed in some confessions of faith. Theologically, it has often reinforced overwhelming dependence of humans on God's power for liberation, maintaining the utter depravity of humanity. The "Latin" reliance on legal images permeates presentations of justification as God making us righteous through the pronouncement of innocence, despite our human guilt as sinners. Again, the differentiation between God's power to make human beings righteous on the one hand, and the human need and unworthiness for such benevolent judgment on the other hand results in setting up a sharp contrast between God and humans. The "subjective" type is the most humanistic of the three, and reflects a Christian ethos of morality. Jesus serves as the example of this, and our response ought to be one which is full of awe and humble gratitude. Humanity is encouraged to do the best it can, knowing all the while that it can do very little.

What remains constant throughout Aulén's typology is the centrality and value of Jesus' death. This is a constant of atonement theory as we have seen it, and this presentation of it is reinforcement. Whether it be spoken of in terms of God delivering humanity, Jesus paying some satisfaction to God, or a spiritual conversion in the face of such a great sacrifice on our behalf, atonement is fundamentally about how we understand Jesus' death bringing humanity into a reconciled relationship with God. That it does is a presumption of Christian theology.

Scholars have noted that this typology depends on and reflects some of Aulén's own presumptions about the incarnation and its relationship to the atonement; thus his assessment of thinkers like Anselm and Luther is challenged. "Ultimately, then, Aulén's criterion for the assessment of theories of the atonement is a particular understanding of the incarnation and its purpose."[13] This understanding has to do with the continuity between the two, and leads to the suggestion that Aulén emphasizes the divinity of Jesus Christ to the exclusion of his humanity. Eugene Fairweather insists that as far as Anselm was concerned, the incarnate one was fully God and fully human, and the unity of the two natures in one person was the means for salvation. "No doubt Aulén is right in seeing in the whole story the triumph of God over the powers of evil, but he goes desperately wrong in failing to recognize

---

[13] Eugene R. Fairweather, "Incarnation and Atonement: An Anselmian Response to Aulén's *Christus Victor,*" *CJT* 7 (1961) 169.

that the very heart of this divine triumph is the conquest of sin by the perfect human obedience of the Word made flesh."[14] He tries here to return the conversation to emphasize the humanity of Jesus which was the vehicle for salvation, not just the divinity of the victorious Christ.

A particular line of criticism has been leveled against Aulén as he associates Luther with the "classic" view of atonement:

> Its central theme is the idea of the Atonement as a Divine conflict and victory; Christ—Christus Victor—fights against and triumphs over the evil powers of the world, the 'tyrants' under which mankind is in bondage and suffering, and in Him God reconciles the world to Himself.[15]

Aulén devotes much time to Luther and the Latin view, with which Luther had been associated, suggesting instead that we understand Luther's teaching as a "revival of the old classic theme of the Atonement as taught by the Fathers, but with a greater depth of treatment."[16] He suggests that God's triumph over evil in Christ is the central affirmation of Luther. Scholars disagree that this 'victory' is the complete basis for the restored relationship between God and the human being in Luther's thought.

Paul Althaus states that Aulén's reading of Luther is unsubstantiated, particularly in terms of the origins of the powers which Christ fights against. Returning to what we have already learned about Luther's understanding of God, Althaus emphasizes that "the powers with which Christ struggles had their power and authority only through God's wrath. They are his instruments against the sinner."[17] These are not powers from outside of the realm and powers of God, rather they originate from the wrath of God, they represent God's *opus alienum* (alien work) and have their place with the law as what Althaus refers to as "enemy of man." It is important to note that Althaus shows how Luther diverges from the strictly dualistic good force/evil force model. In matters of the atonement at least, that which Christ struggles against is the wrath of God—the means by which God uses law in relationship to the sinner.

This point of Althaus' is challenged by Heiko Oberman, who places Luther's view of human life in the world very much in the midst of conflict between God and the Devil.

---

[14] Ibid., 175.

[15] *Christus Victor*, 20.

[16] Ibid., 118.

[17] Paul Althaus, *The Theology of Martin Luther,* trans. Robert C. Schultz (Philadelphia: Fortress, 1966) 220.

Luther's phraseology and imagery—"joyful exchange" and "Jacob's ladder"—are totally devoid of any trace of abstract academic sterility. They express life in process and not a static condition; they originate from the living experience of faith in a life between God and the Devil, not from theological theory.[18]

Oberman is very clear that the devil is a real figure in Luther's theology. Human life itself must be conceived in this manner, and this gives a whole new dimension to the idea of struggle, and of life in process or on the move ("*eine Lebens-Bewegung aus, nicht einen Zustand*"). Human life is not static and living between God and the devil is the key characteristic of it in Oberman's assessment. These matters are of life and death as far as the human being is concerned, and God is the one who is working against the devil to protect and preserve humanity. He states that faith is in a God who "*der unter dem Kreuzezeichen um eine Welt streitet, die ihm der Teufel streitig macht.*"[19] (Under the symbol of the cross, God is fighting for a world which the devil is trying to win.)

This presents some of the conflict metaphor that Aulén tried to associate with Luther. Ted Peters agrees that the conflict/victory themes are very much present in Luther's thought on the atonement and the life of Christ. However, he faults Aulén for failing to present and appreciate the complexity of Luther's theology. "Aulén has supplied us with an accurate presentation of the Christus Victor motif in Luther's christology. But he goes astray when he attempts to make a case for holding that this theory is the only one Luther propounded."[20] Peters suggests that satisfaction is also a part of the way Luther understands the atonement, and shows how it is related to the Christus Victor motif. "For Luther satisfaction includes the notion of penal substitution. Christ suffers our punishment."[21] Peters argument against Aulén is that Luther's thought reflects much more than just the victory motif, and it includes a consistent and thoughtful consideration of the relationship between God's forgiveness of humanity and the role of Christ's work.

Regarding Luther's theory of the atonement and Christ's work, Althaus says: "The satisfaction which God's righteousness demands constitutes the primary and decisive significance of Christ's work and particularly of his

---

[18] Heiko Oberman. *Luther: Man between God and the Devil*, trans. Eileen Walliser-Schwarzbart (New Haven: Yale University Press, 1989) 185.

[19] German texts from Oberman, *Luther: Mensch zwischen Gott und Teufel* (Berlin: Severin und Siedler, 1983) 196, 166.

[20] Ted Peters, "The Atonement in Anselm and Luther, Second Thoughts about Gustaf Aulén's Christus Victor," *LQ* 24 (1972) 309.

[21] Ibid., 310.

death. Everything else depends on this satisfaction, including the destruction of the might and the authority of the demonic powers."[22]

The point of this distinction is to understand Christ as priest and king, who protects the sinner and works to intercede for us with God. This comes together with the imagery of destroying the demonic powers. Further, Althaus insists that Luther protects the power of God as the source for even those things which are associated with the demonic. This is the wrath of God, the function of the law, and the hiddenness of the divine which is fully characteristic of Luther's theology. This is the *opus alienum*, and one way that the otherness of God is explored.

In all of this conversation about atonement theory and theological interpretations of it, some general themes remain. Something is done on the cross that brings humanity to be in right relationship with God. Humanity is in a sort of bondage (to the world, to the devil) and depends upon the (perfect) obedience of the (perfect) Son in order to be restored to relationship with God. The themes of satisfaction, substitution, sacrifice, obedience, punishment and guilt guide traditional theories. These ideas have implications for our concept of God. Criticism of Aulén's typology perpetuates these themes, albeit with nuanced differences. Assumptions about God and the human being remain throughout.

This book asks the questions about the characters of God and the human being in this relationship reflected in atonement: What does it imply for our concept of God when Anselm insists that something is demanded in order to restore a human's relationship with God? What did human beings do that severed their relationship with God? What does it mean when Abelard suggests that the way we are brought to full spiritual conversion is through reflection on the death of Jesus? This is the point at which the critical voices from contemporary theology will come in. Other contemporary theological reflection on the atonement continues in the line of thought which we have seen presented here.

Atonement Themes: To the Present

Contemporary theologians continue to wrestle with the questions that have occupied those working on issues of atonement. Some retain general traditional assertions about the atonement, and their work will help us to clarify the themes pertaining to the relationship between God and the human being with which we have been concerned. Contemporary Lutheran theologian Gerhard Forde puts it this way:

---

[22] Althaus, *The Theology of Martin Luther*, 220.

> Atonement is done to us. The resurrection of the crucified One means death and life for us. If the event, the accident, happens to us, breaks into our lives with the impact we have been trying to describe, then it will involve a full stop and a new beginning: a death of the old and the resurrection of the new in faith.[23]

The connection between death and new life draws from Luther's theology: The need for death to an old life, and the activity of Jesus Christ as the means by which we as human beings are made to live a new life in the presence of God connects specifically with Luther's construction of baptism as the way that we are drowned to sin and raised up in Christ. The need for suffering and death in order to have life in Christ is a crucial theme here, and it is affirmed in Forde's interpretation of atonement. "The reason is precisely that the cross means death and new life. The old subject is not just given an example to follow, or inspiration to encourage its flagging religious ambitions. The old subject dies and a new one is called into being in Jesus by faith."[24]

We can see here a direct criticism of the "subjective" type of atonement which has been linked with Abelard. Forde insists that it is not merely an example, but that something actually happens to the human being as a result of the death and new life found on the cross. The death of the old person and the life of the new person with God in Christ through faith is effected through atonement. As we saw in Luther's sacramental theology, this cycle of death and rebirth is an important part of understanding the events of the cross—the events of what Forde calls "actual atonement."

Some theologians place the death of Jesus within a culture and a world that used sacrifice as a means to appease God's wrath or to gain favor from God. Millard Erickson refers to Leviticus 4:35, where we find reference to the priest burning an offering on the fire to make atonement for the sin committed, so that forgiveness might be provided, and asks the question: "Can there be any doubt, especially in view of God's anger against sin, that this verse points to an appeasement of God? How else can we interpret the statement that the offering should be made to the Lord and forgiveness would follow?"[25] Erickson seeks to understand the culture of sacrifice in which Jesus found himself. This is one way to get to his understanding that God required/requested/wanted the death of Jesus in order to restore a fallen humanity to relationship with the divine. The theme of sacrifice in atonement theory is here based on a cultural norm of making an offering to god on behalf of the

---

[23] Gerhard O. Forde, "The Work of Christ: Atonement as Actual Event," in *Christian Dogmatics,* ed. Carl E. Braaten and Robert W. Jenson (Philadelphia: Fortress, 1984) 2:95.

[24] Ibid.

[25] Millard Erickson, *Christian Theology* (Grand Rapids: Baker, 1983) 812.

human community. Erickson carries this through atonement, insisting that the death of Jesus was that offering to God which brought about he forgiveness of sins. Sacrifice as a continuing theme of atonement theory will be critically examined in the next section of this chapter.

While Erickson attempts to retain the sacrificial theme of atonement, Anthony Tambasco suggests that Paul's model of the atonement be used to understand the life and the death of Jesus. "Presently we shall suggest that Paul's model may be better described as a representative journey in which the risen Christ invites us to participate."[26] In this way, Tambasco suggests that we not isolate the death of Jesus on the cross as an event which in and of itself redeems all of humanity. This, he suggests, is the fault of Anselm's model of the atonement, and one which can be reexamined in terms of its appropriateness. The solution is to understand Jesus' death as sacrifice of his life, a gift to God on behalf of all humanity. Ultimately, it is this: "Atonement is God's action and humanity's cooperation in reuniting humanity with God through union with Christ, whose blood released in death is sacrificial symbol of his life fully joined to God."[27] It is important to see that while Tambasco attempts to remove the suffering and death of Jesus on the cross from isolation, and affirm the importance of his life and work, the sacrifice which is made remains a thematic driving point of the atonement. Atonement is God's action.

Tambasco, like Forde, retains the thematic significance of death and new life: "Participation in the risen life of Christ, however, is participation also in his suffering and death. Paul says this in verse 10 where, literally, 'that I may share his sufferings' is translated, 'that I may know the fellowship of his sufferings.'"[28] This inescapable association of new life with death returns us to a fundamental problem of atonement theory which we have been naming. In order to come into life with Christ, right relationship with God, the death of the perfect son is necessary. Even if his death on the cross was not necessary, it simply is the means by which Christian theologians have said that humanity is restored to relationship with God. Participation in the suffering of Jesus is the way in which humanity shares in his risen life. All of this affects and is affected by our understanding of the relationship between the human being and God.

Colin Gunton says: "The three metaphors of atonement take their meaning, when understood in depth, from relationships."[29] When he exam-

---

[26] Anthony J. Tambasco, *A Theology of Atonement and Paul's Vision of Christianity* (Collegeville, Minn.: Liturgical, 1991) 66.

[27] Ibid., 70.

[28] *A Theology of the Atonement*, 63.

[29] Colin Gunton, *The Actuality of Atonement: A Study of Metaphor, Rationality and the Christian Tradition* (Edinburgh: T. & T. Clark, 1988) 143.

ines the themes of victory, justice, and sacrifice, he speaks of the fundamental ways in which we view the relationship between God and the human being. Atonement, defined as the event which brings humanity and God into right relationship again, forces us to ask the questions of how, why, and so on. "[The metaphors] reveal that the problem which the atonement engages is . . . a disrupted relationship with the creator . . . . [T]here needs be a rec-reative, redemptive divine initiative in which the root of the problem, the disrupted personal relationship, is set to rights."[30] Gunton here affirms the point we have been making about atonement: it is fundamentally about the relationship between God and the human being. It forces us to look at the partners in the relationship, and the gifts and deficiencies that each brings to the covenant. However, while making that point, he continues in the line of Christian theology we have seen which states that God's initiative alone can bring about the reconciliation. This is once and only through the cross "with Jesus taking our place before God . . . ."[31]

It is the *need* for death in order to bring about life is that which is questioned most deeply through this project. It is firmly present in Anselm's writings. It is also the fact that Jesus' death on the cross *is* taken to be the moment of reconciliation between God and humanity. This is firmly present in most theological reflection on the atonement. Further, the association of suffering and death with new life and reconciliation with God remains a crucial part of the discussions of atonement we have examined thus far. Whether or not we affirm that the death of Jesus on the cross was necessary, traditional Christian theology continues to try to explicate the "fact" that through the death of Jesus humanity and God have been reconciled. The themes we have examined thusfar include God's need for Jesus death in order to restore a fallen humanity, the power of Jesus' life and death on the cross for spiritual conversion, Jesus' death as a part of sacrifice culture which understood the meaning of his offering, the centrality of suffering and death for speaking about the relationship between God and the human being, and the cycle of death and rebirth.

Did Jesus live only that he might die to save humanity? Was Jesus' death a ransom for our guilt or a substitution for the punishment we deserved? Did Jesus sacrifice himself or did God demand his death? Was there need, as Anselm suggested, for satisfaction to be paid to God, in order for God to get the honor due Him? It is important to analyze the implications of these proposals for understanding atonement. The fact is that whatever happens in the details of atonement theory, the life, death, and resurrection of Jesus *is the*

---

[30] Ibid., 160.
[31] Ibid., 167.

means by which humanity comes to be in right relation with God. Even more specifically, it is the death of Jesus that is the celebrated moment in the life of the church. What are the consequences of a theology whose pivotal events are the cross, the tortured death of a man who sought to teach the word of God?

From Atonement back to Jesus: Life, Ministry, and Criticism

Feminist Criticism and Feminist Responses

The death of Jesus as Christ is the pivotal event in atonement theory. Simply stated, it is through his suffering and death on the cross that God brings about salvation and right relationship between the divine and the human. Therefore, the cross is an essential aspect of Christian theology. It even serves as sort of a filter through which all things about God and the human being and the relationship between the two are understood. Luther insists that to be a theologian means to be a theologian of the cross, to know God is to know Christ on the cross.[32] Here is where we as humans encounter God most fully. In the preceding section of this chapter, we saw the ways in which theologians have reflected on atonement as the event which reconciled God and humanity. The implications of centralizing suffering, death, and the cross within Christian theology have been criticized most particularly by feminist theologians in the contemporary era. Some of these theologians argue that this perceived or real theological justification of suffering can lead to a social acceptance of violence and abuse.

> Christianity is an abusive theology that glorifies suffering. Is it any wonder that there is so much abuse in modern society when the predominant image of theology of the culture is of 'divine child abuse'— God the Father demanding and carrying out the suffering and death of his own son? If Christianity is to be liberating for the oppressed, it must itself be liberated from this theology.[33]

This chapter aims to address this critical turn. Liberation of western Christianity from potentially destructive atonement theories is essential to this reformation of theology as it is concerned with human life in community, and in relationship with God.

---

[32] See Luther's treatise "The Heidelberg Disputation," (1518) in *LW* 31:35–70.
[33] Joanne Carlson Brown and Rebecca Parker, "For God So Loved the World?," in *Christianity, Patriarchy, and Abuse: A Feminist Critique*, ed. Joanne Carlson Brown and Carole R. Bohn (Cleveland: Pilgrim, 1989) 26.

Brown and Parker's statement has become a major statement of one powerful strain of feminist theological criticism of the Christian theory of the atonement.[34] It suggests that there is first a connection between the theological and the social. It suggests further that the symbol of the cross and the events and theologies surrounding it emphasize the salvific effects of suffering in such a way that it presents violence and suffering in a positive light. This is then brought into an already overwhelmingly abusive culture. It posits God as the powerful Father, translated as the abusive patriarch seen too often in this culture, who satisfies His need through the death of His own Son. The claim being made is that if God does this, then it theologically justifies human domination and abuse. The charge is serious, and it relies in part on these connections between theological images and social realities. One presumption of feminist theology is the need to take women's experience seriously, and the fact is that women have been very often on the underside of various power struggles throughout history. This positioning allows the feminist theologian to be intensely aware of the dangerous implications of theological models for social structures.

The above statement serves as a major impetus for this book and has served as the nagging question in the back of my mind ever since I participated in the summer conference on the atonement mentioned in the introduction. The sheer difference between the positions of Brown and Parker, and the Lutheran theologians like Juel and Forde, leaves an indelible mark on my view of atonement and theology. What does this mean for me if I am to be a theologian within the Lutheran tradition? It means that I have to reckon with both. I have attempted to get to the issues by going to the fundamental way in which we understand the relationship between God and the human being, believing that if we can adjust the way we understand the relationship, we can adjust the way we understand atonement. Through an examination and reframing of this relationship based on human agency and divine mutuality, we are enabled now to return to the critical statement and assess its importance and its limitations. Other feminist theologians have also taken this charge of divine child abuse seriously, and have attempted to answer it in different ways.

Leanne VanDyk suggests that proposing a model of divine child abuse violates authentic trinitarian doctrine, and proposes that an understanding of God as Trinity based on mutuality protects Christian theology from this charge.

---

[34] See also Rita Nakashima Brock, *Journeys By Heart: A Christology of Erotic Power* (New York: Crossroad, 1988).

> A Trinity doctrine with images of mutuality and a common divine graciousness shields atonement theology from egregious misunderstandings and misuses. Specifically, a trinitarian doctrine with these characteristics renders incomprehensible the charge that atonement is divine child abuse.[35]

VanDyk suggests that Christian theology, based on the concept of a triune God, implies the understanding of mutuality and graciousness among the persons of the trinity and between God and the world. Unfortunately, it is not the case that such mutuality and graciousness have been always present in theological reflection on the atonement, or on God, or on the human being. We have seen this reflected in the traditional voices examined thus far. Her argument against the validity of any charge of divine child abuse best serves as a suggestion for future theological construction—that we take seriously the implications of a triune God, and that we delve deep into this model and its implications for understanding divine mutuality, and human reciprocity.

Thelma Megill-Cobbler suggests that we look at atonement theory in such a way as to reassess the "blame" and to move away from charging God with wrongdoing.

> A possible short answer to the charge of divine child abuse would be to point out that it was Herod, not God, who was responsible for the slaughter of the innocents; that the intended victim of that story is a survivor who later walks on the path to the cross with a wholeness and freedom that does not banish anguish and doubt.[36]

This echoes Abelard's shift toward assessing some human blame for the death of Jesus. Megill-Cobbler rightly assigns blame for human deaths to the human beings in this world, not to God as divine child abuser. She stops just short of connecting Herod's slaughter of the innocents as a mirror to Jesus' death on the cross, but we are certainly enabled to do just that. She portrays Jesus as a survivor of that slaughter who confidently walks down the path of his life. She also says that leads to the cross. Does this serve us in a constructive manner when it comes to the questions about God? Megill-Cobbler suggests that we not blame God, because it ultimately is the people involved who bring about the unjust death.

But where and who is God in relation to those persons? And what does it mean that Herod ordered the slaughter of the innocents, or that someone ordered the crucifixion of Jesus? Certainly Jesus survived once, perhaps by the grace of God, but his life does end on the cross. Megill-Cobbler proposes that

---

[35] Leanne VanDyk, "Do Theories of Atonement Foster Abuse?" *Dialog* 35 (1996) 24.

[36] Thelma Megill-Cobbler, "A Feminist Rethinking of Punishment Imagery in Atonement," *Dialog* 35 (1996) 20.

our conversations about the cross ought to further our conversation about the reality of unjust suffering in the world. "If the cross is the judgment of God upon human sin, it reveals *all* our violence and pretensions."[37] The brokenness of the cross is a part of our world, and Megill-Cobbler appropriately views it as a statement against the world. However, she maintains the image of the relationship between God and the human being we have been finding throughout atonement theory: "The courtroom analogy suggests that our situation in relation to God is desperate, that God's intentions for the creation have been violated, and that the violation which has entered the human scene is not something God will ignore."[38] The imagery of judge and criminal remains, and the power dynamic is clearly set. Megill-Cobbler attempts to reframe the image by suggesting that in Jesus, God the benevolent judge steps over the bench and takes the place of the criminal and accepts her punishment. However, this continues to assume that God's offense at the violation within creation must be appeased, that something must be done on behalf of humanity in order to restore right relationship.

Darby Ray begins her exploration of the atonement with some of the same attention to violation and evil within creation: "the issue of atonement is the issue of confronting human evil. It poses the crucial question of whether, and how, human beings can be redeemed from our own evil and reconciled to God and the rest of the world."[39] The underlying theme of this is the relationship between God and the human being. How is it brought about, maintained, and restored? Ray further suggests, in addressing the charges of divine child abuse, that theologians, feminist theologians in particular, not abandon the entire notion of atonement. Rather, she suggests that we use conversation about the atonement as the means by which we can seriously address the presence of evil in the world, and God's response to it.

> Taking evil seriously, as the patristic model of atonement does, means that we recognize its reality and power, admitting that within this finite, fragile world, good and evil are locked in battle, that moral existence has the character of struggle, and that it is up to us to keep hope alive by loving and living the good and resisting evil in concrete acts of compassion and celebration.[40]

In her argument to reappropriate what she calls the patristic model of the atonement, Ray affirms the crucial importance of understanding ourselves

---

[37] Ibid.

[38] Ibid., 19.

[39] Darby Kathleen Ray, *Deceiving the Devil: Atonement, Abuse, and Ransom* (Cleveland: Pilgrim, 1998) 6.

[40] Ibid., 133.

as human beings in the world, of struggling against those evils which we encounter in life, and of affirming God's presence in the struggle. The details of her proposal suggest that the patristic, or "fishhook," model of the atonement is one that can be demythologized to demonstrate God's creativity and cunning in struggling against the reality of evil in the world.

This proposal is helpful in the way it confronts the reality of evil and violence within the world, and the way in which is works with the reality of struggle and the need for hope. The problem with it remains a problem with this type of atonement theory *per se*. The imagery of cosmic battle between good and evil remains, with victory and defeat as outcomes. Ray suggests that the model which posits Jesus as a sort of lure for the devil exposes the fraudulent claims of the devil on humanity. "The devil actually causes his own defeat by overstepping his boundaries, making an idol of his power, ignoring his limits, assuming he can have what is not his."[41] The deception that dangles Jesus on a "fishhook" as bait, she suggests, requires God's creativity and understanding of the situation in order to bring about the best possible result. Ray frames these issues within liberation theologies which take seriously struggle within the world and the need for creativity in order for survival. However, it remains troubling in that God is presented as master manipulator, and Jesus is put in danger and is killed as a part of the greater scheme of salvation.

The charge and the responses all coming from feminist theologians leave the questions of atonement open, and remind us that there is no easy way to get at these complex issues. To take the charge seriously means that we take the reality of an abusive and oppressive society seriously. To answer the charge demands that the theologian work out for herself the interplay between tradition and experience, between history and the present. The three feminist theologians we have seen here, VanDyk, Megill-Cobbler, and Ray, all present alternatives and answers to the charge of divine child abuse that get at different parts of the problem. VanDyk moves in the direction of affirming mutual relationality as a fundamental characteristic of God. Megill-Cobbler gets to the issue of human culpability for the death of Jesus. Ray locates the problems within the realm of theodicy: Where is God in the face of human suffering? These theologians do not fully address the issues of atonement theory, however. We will continue to bring in other contemporary theological proposals in attempt to put together a proposal.

---

[41] Ibid., 140.

Hefner: From Sacrifice to the Created Co-Creator

Now that we have examined the character of some charges against Christian atonement theory, and seen some of the ways in which feminist theologians in particular are wrestling with the questions and attempting to discern some answers, we can move to discussing some more ways in which theologians are working with models of christology and atonement in ways that serve the liberation and emancipation that is understood to be the vision of God. We briefly encountered sacrifice as a theme of atonement theory. Philip Hefner revisits this notion in a way that he intends to revive the value of sacrifice so that it can be understood to make it viable today. He also works out of the notion of a created co-creator, to which we were introduced in chapter one, in such a way that reevaluates the meaning and impact of the life and death of Jesus as Christ.

First, regarding sacrifice, Hefner proposes that the biblical image of sacrifice has a power and a relevance that is too often dismissed. The dangers of masochism and violence are duly noted, but it is emphasized that these social tendencies are not a part of the biblical tradition. Sacrifice in his argument is four main things:

> First . . . it is an intentional service, possibly unto death if need be, which is an assertion and fulfillment of the self . . . . Second, sacrifice aims not at violence, but at reconciliation, covenant belonging, peace, and healing. Third, sacrifice is a psychologically and socially profound symbol which holds in creative balance human and divine activity and receptivity . . . . Finally, . . . it is the action of strong persons who have focused the meaning of their lives.[42]

Through this proposed way of thinking about sacrifice, Hefner is responding to the question: How do I make my life count? It is clear that with this in mind, he intends to posit the death of Jesus as an intentional activity, undertaken with a firmness of conviction and identity, ("unto death if need be") which demonstrates the power of the human and the graciousness of the divine. This is how Jesus' life counts. These are arguments that I find to be theologically provocative, and indeed am in accord with in terms of developing the agency of the human being, and Jesus as being exemplary of such definitive statement of identity and action for purposes of liberation.

However, this fails to get at the most crucial questions surrounding the life and death of Jesus that we have seen raised in our analysis of atonement theory. Suggesting that sacrifice be a concept that is accepted and lifted up as a valuable model by which we could theoretically live our lives fails to address

---

[42] Philip Hefner, "The Cultural Significance of Jesus' Death as Sacrifice," *JR* 60 (1980) 420.

the deeper issues which include the need for sacrifice in the first place, and the subtle ways in which sacrifice is held up to be a virtue in many social situations. Certainly in the face of great challenge and in the midst of struggle, individuals make choices that they must live or die with. But what of the larger question of the structural reasons for such threats to life and struggles for well-being? Hefner's proposal perhaps serves well enough as counsel for individuals to deal with present injustice through self-investment and proaction. It fails in questioning the very presence of such injustice, and questioning God's role in being present with and even against those things which threaten life and wholeness in the world. It presumes a strength of character and morality and body which is admirable, but is not always realistic.

I affirm the emphasis on making one's life matter and understanding the life of Jesus as one which made tremendous difference, but I cannot help but resist any proposal which maintains and upholds the very term "sacrifice." For his own purposes, Hefner may have formulated a useful concept of sacrifice, but this concept does not address the main issues of this book, nor does if satisfy our need to reframe atonement theory. We do not live in the midst of the biblical world wherein these notions of identity and intention and covenantal relationship are widely understood and granted. We must take into account the present social and political realm in which human beings live their lives and make their choices on a daily basis. This realm is messy and unfair and brutal and challenging on many levels, as it can be rewarding and liberating and fulfilling on many others. "Sacrifice" need not be a part of either.

Hefner's notion of the created co-creator also contributes to our understanding of Jesus Christ. I find this proposal more compelling and constructive: "Homo sapiens is God's created co-creator, whose purpose is the 'stretching/enabling' of the systems of nature so that they can participate in God's purposes in the mode of freedom, for which the paradigm is Jesus Christ, both in respect to his life and to his understanding of the world as God's creation."[43] As the paradigm of life and freedom, the character of Jesus Christ embodies the vision of God, in and of himself. The point, then, is to understand the incarnation as having the goal of enabling the world to participate in and be receptive to God. The participation in God that characterizes human life is chiefly found in the life of Jesus. This makes a statement not only about human beings, but about God.

In this proposal, we see that God is the goal, in a way, and that God's vision "in the mode of freedom" can be the consummation of creation—its purpose and its goal. God functions more as the lure which we found in the philosophy of Whitehead, than as the controlling dominator which we find

---

[43] Hefner, "Biocultural Evolution and the Created Co-Creator," *Dialog* 36 (1997) 203–4.

in some strains of Christian thought. This radically alters the way in which we view the life of Jesus, his death, and God's presence or role throughout. God is not the transcendent Father demanding payment, satisfaction, or death. God is the persuasive power ever moving the broken world toward a fuller realization of itself. With Megill-Cobbler we can affirm that God's grace is manifest in Jesus' escape from the slaughter of the innocents, but recognize with Ray that the powers of violation and evil make a real impact as in the death of Jesus. We can then see how the resurrection is a manifestation of God's ability to work within the messy reality of the world and bring about the best possible future. We may call this resurrection or new life in Christ or even the strength to continue in faith. God's presence is unfailing, even in face of the cross.

With the emphasis on human agency and divine mutuality, the life and ministry of Jesus become the central aspects of a Christology or atonement theory. The death and resurrection of Jesus become statements about the power of the world as well as the presence of God's power. If we as humans are brought into right-relationship with God through the life and death of Jesus, through his commitment to the vision of God, his embodiment of a life in the vision of God, then the emphasis here can be shifted to the life and ministry of Jesus, the stretching and enabling in which he engaged. He pushed the limits of the world in which he lived, in order to "make room" for the realm/kingdom/vision of God. The means to right-relationship are thus found in the processes of life itself. While it is a big and important part of the story that this very stretching of the world, pushing it beyond itself, snapped back on Jesus and resulted in his death on the cross, it is not the whole story. God envisions humanity within the world processes, within life-giving moments, as being the co-creators and the enablers of fulfilling creation.

"Feminist" Constructive Options: Jesus, Surrogacy, and Justice

Violence and violation as they are imaged and approved or celebrated in Jesus translate to the human community in particular ways. This is the connection between the theological and the social which we saw in Brown and Parker's statement. Delores Williams engages Christian doctrine and atonement theory in order to show how the presentation of Jesus in Christian theology has often undermined its own liberating potential to reinforce social stereotypical roles of subjugation and surrogacy. "In this sense, Jesus represents the ultimate surrogate figure; he stands in the place of someone else: sinful humankind.... If black women accept this idea of redemption, can they not also passively accept the exploitation that surrogacy brings?"[44] It is this exploitation of black

---

[44] Delores S. Williams, *Sisters in the Wilderness: The Challenge of Womanist God-Talk* (Mary-

women that Williams takes seriously in her construction of a womanist theology. Theological doctrine that reinforces social subjugation is not to be accepted, and ought to be critically engaged and deeply examined. Atonement as substitution is the particular type of theory with which Williams takes issue here. This is a popular and dominant way of viewing atonement in many churches today, and she insists that it reinforces social stereotypical roles that are destructive to black women.

Williams seeks to reframe the christological conversation with these things in mind, and insists that theology reflect the affirmation that "God did not intend the surrogacy roles they [black women] have been forced to perform."[45] God is a God of liberation from enslavement, not a God who orders, approves, or allows suffering to have the last and definitive word about the world. Therefore, she states that "Jesus did not come to be a surrogate."[46] Rather, he came to actualize something about God, and to teach the world about the grace of the divine. Williams calls this the ministerial vision:

> Jesus showed humankind a vision of righting relations between body, mind and spirit *through an ethical ministry of words . . . a healing ministry of touch . . . a militant ministry of expelling evil . . . a ministry grounded in the power of faith . . . a ministry of prayer . . . a ministry of compassion and love.* Humankind is, then, redeemed through Jesus's *ministerial* vision of life and not through his death.[47]

Her proposal here is that we fully and completely understand the power of the life and the ministry of Jesus as redemptive, and that we move away from the redemptive significance of surrogacy, suffering on the cross, and dying for a greater good. We can see how this moves Christian thought further in the direction that Abelard once suggested. Williams' analysis is contextualized within a womanist commitment that takes seriously the experience of black women in the North American context, in a society wherein men and white women have utilized the bodies and souls of black women for their own, purportedly greater, purposes.

The power of Williams' proposal is this move toward detailing the redemptive significance of Jesus' life as an alternate to substitutionary atonement theory. The "ministerial vision" which she upholds speaks to the power of life, the processed through which humankind moves in their relationships to the world and ultimately to God. This mission of Jesus incorporates teaching the mind, healing the body, dealing with evil, believing in God, and

knoll, N.Y.: Orbis, 1993) 162.
[45] Ibid., 166.
[46] Ibid., 167.
[47] Ibid.

caring for the other. As a vision, this is what God intends for humanity. This is the vision that God has for the world, and human beings are to be the partners in bringing the vision to light: The mission of Jesus is the vision of God.

Beverly Harrison ties her vision of human agency which we examined in chapter two to re-visioning the life and work of Jesus. It is important to emphasize human freedom and creativity as a means for empowerment. "It is necessary to open up the naturalistic metaphors for God to the power of human activity, to freedom not only as radical creativity but also as radical moral power."[48] This follows her analysis of Mary Daly's challenge to reevaluate classic ontology, and to open up the category of being so that we can understand the radical creative power in the experience of women—as Be-ing. Her point is to establish the connections between human experience and conception of God, and the way in which Jesus comes to embody some of each.

In her understanding of the life and ministry of Jesus, Harrison relies on an understanding of otherworldliness not as escapism, but as encouraging "an ongoing struggle against the present order by conjuring a better time and a better place, beyond the oppressive here and now."[49] Here is where her construction of human agency "fleshes out" the way in which she understands the ministry of Jesus. It is precisely this struggle against the present order in which Jesus engaged. The struggle is undergone with the "better time and better place" envisioned by God in mind for the world. In attempting to live in accord with the liberating transforming vision of God in the world, Jesus was in conflict with the prevailing moral and social order. This is important to understand as it has implications for discerning the reasons for Jesus' death.

His life, Harrison proposes, is an "active embodiment of love," and is not to be understood as a "headlong race toward Golgotha, toward crucifixion." His suffering and death was not the only way to restore God and humanity to right relation. Harrison affirms: "His death was the price he paid for refusing to abandon the radical activity of love—of expressing solidarity and reciprocity with the excluded ones in his community."[50] He died on that cross because the persons invested in that present order refused to allow his vision of mutuality and human fulfillment in God to take full effect. This proposal frames the issue of the cross, and of the life and death of Jesus in a way that refuses to allow justification and rationalization for the virtue of torture and, yes, sacrifice:

---

[48] Beverly Harrison, "The Power of Anger and the Work of Love," in *Making the Connections: Essays in Feminist Social Ethics*, edited by Carol S. Robb (Boston: Beacon, 1985) 10.

[49] Ibid., 6.

[50] Ibid., 18.

> Sacrifice, I submit, is not a central moral goal or virtue in the Christian life. Radical acts of love—expressing human solidarity and bringing mutual relationship to life—are the central virtues of the Christian moral life. That we have turned sacrifice into a moral virtue has deeply confused the Christian moral tradition.[51]

Harrison affirms that Jesus accepted what was to be the sacrifice of his life, but this was more the result of a regretful risk of being faithful than the result of intentionally chosen death.

Her final call is to move from the virtue of sacrifice to the actions of mutuality and solidarity, expressing, embodying, sharing, and celebrating the gift of life. We ought to seek to right wrong relations, whether that be among humans, between human beings and the world, between the world and God, or any other distorted relationship in the realm of life that gives opportunity for violation or violence. The work of love, as she describes it, must seek to end crucifixions and the need for sacrifice, no matter how you understand the term. If one "ends up" dying, like Jesus did, then that is a tragic statement about the world first and foremost. If that death serves as any impetus for the surrounding community's outrage or deepened commitment, then God's grace is manifest in the responses. This does not excuse or ignore the tragic nature of the world which brings about such deaths in the first place. Nevertheless, the work of love must find the strength to continue.

As we briefly examined the theology of Elizabeth Johnson in the earlier discussion of God's presence in the world as Sophia, we were led to the point at which she affirms the presence and reality of Jesus as God-with-us: "Sophia pitches her tent in the midst of the world."[52] Johnson locates her feminist analysis within the tradition of feminist theologians who are taking the notion of Christology to task for enforcing and reinforcing patriarchal ideals of maleness and divinity. "If Jesus is a man, so uncritical reasoning goes, and as such the revelation of God, then this must point to maleness as an essential characteristic of divine being itself."[53] Again, we ought to note that Johnson, as a Roman Catholic woman, starts her conversation about the person of Jesus at the point at which the Roman Catholic church has used it and continues to use it to exclude women from ordained leadership in the church, and to suggest its images for God within a male-oriented world. Gender is an issue, because it has traditionally been made an issue within the Roman Catholic context.

---

[51] Ibid.

[52] Elizabeth A. Johnson, *She Who Is: The Mystery of God in Feminist Theological Discourse* (New York: Crossroad, 1992) 150.

[53] Ibid., 152.

The person of Jesus becomes, for Johnson, the primary way in which human beings can understand God's relationship to the world, and God's valuation of the human. "[I]t also evokes Sophia's characteristic gracious goodness, life-giving creativity, and passion for justice as key hermeneutical elements in speaking about the mission of Jesus."[54] It is this mission of Jesus through which we are to understand the character of Sophia, God who has a passion and a drive toward justice and emancipation, who lives that out in the midst of the human community through word and through action. The mission of Jesus is the vision of God: "Through his ministry Jesus unleashes a hope, a vision, and a present experience of liberating relationships that women, the lowest of the low in any class, as well as men, savor as the antithesis of patriarchy."[55] This embodies the vision of God: liberating relationship and mutual respect, compassion and boldness. The way in which Jesus lives these things out in the world, through his relationships, serves as more than a paradigm for human be-ing. It is, as Harrison calls for, a paradigm for human Do-ing.

Johnson argues that Sophia-God unites with humanity in the world, "in incarnation and suffering" and "shows that the passion of God is clearly directed toward the lifting of oppression and the establishing of right relations."[56] She says that God entered into human history in a manner that intended our liberation from the powers of destruction and oppression. The person of Jesus and the stories of his life work become the way in which we connect with and comprehend the meaning for our lives and the presence of God to us. "She becomes flesh, choosing the very stuff of the cosmos as her own personal reality forever."[57] We can clearly see Johnson's insistence on maintaining Sophia-God's valuation of the physical, fleshly, embodiedness of human life, and the commitment to salvation and transformation that this demonstrates. It simultaneously acknowledges the reality of evil and distortion in the world, in our relationships and our identities, while uplifting the fact that the divine became incarnate, participating in the messiness, and ultimately getting caught up in the middle of a huge mess.

Rather than being the one who punishes humanity for inadequacies, or one who demands something in order to bring about right relationship, God as Sophia engages the world in her divine graciousness and with and for her vision of divine justice. If we are shifting from speaking of human be-ing to human do-ing, then we can see how Johnson speaks of God as not only the foundation and principle of Being, but as the origin of the drive toward

---

[54] Ibid., 157.
[55] Ibid.
[56] Ibid., 166.
[57] Ibid., 168.

justice. Mary Daly suggests that we understand God as Verb, much like what this argument suggests: ". . . as participation in God the Verb who cannot be broken down simply into past, present, and future time, since God is form-destroying, form-creating, transforming power that makes all things new."[58] The point is to fully comprehend that God, as Verb or Sophia, engages the world, engages in the world, and by Her very presence moves/lures the world to a fuller appreciation of life and love, thereby moving/luring the human being to act accordingly. As Harrison says, we are to love- and to act-each-other-into-well-being.

One Final Return to the Philosophical

It may seem odd to return to the philosophy of Kant at this point in the book, but I believe that the concept discussed with the categorical imperative earlier in the project holds some provocative potential for this attempt to reframe our understanding of Jesus' life and the meaning of his death and power of his resurrection. "Man [sic], however, is not a thing, and this not something to be used merely as a means; he must always be regarded in all his actions as an end in himself."[59] If we take this idea and apply it to our attempts to understand the human, paradigmatically seen in Jesus, then we are moved to view his life and his mission in a different light. Jesus as Christ must not be thought of as a means to some greater purpose: his death may not be justified by the greater good which may have come out of it through the grace of God. Likewise, any death which is a "result" of one's commitment to a struggle and intentional activity may not be justified by the subsequent flurry of activity that may follow it.

To speak of Jesus as an end in himself means that we can not merely regard his life and death as a means to our salvation. That Christians believe that they are means is not disputed, but that this is all that the life, ministry, suffering, and death of Jesus mean for us today is a poor reading of a powerful story. As Harrison illustrates, his activity of love, his commitment to the vision of God, was vital and crucial in itself. It is here that we must locate meaning. If the life of Jesus is to have meaning and value in and of itself, then it must be held up as not a mere precursor to the events of the cross, but as an important way of being human, of relating to God, and of actualizing the vision of God.

---

[58] Mary Daly, *Beyond God the Father: Toward a Philosophy of Women's Liberation* (Boston: Beacon, 1973) 43.
[59] Immanuel Kant, "Foundations of the Metaphysics of Morals," (1785) trans. Lewis White Beck (Englewood Cliffs: Prentice Hall, 1990) 46.

Only when we do this, we can affirm, with Harrison, that his death, in and of itself, was an unfortunate and wrong turn of events. It was not an illusion, and it was not automatically perceived that God would bring life out of this death. The blood flowed, the people mourned, and the women went to the tomb. We must not move quickly through the cross on the way to a happier resurrection, as we must not move through the life and ministry to the horrors of the cross. Though these things are all part of one life, each facet of the story of Christology and the elements of an atonement theory must be understood not as a means to the greater end, but appreciated and known in itself, as it plays a role in human experience of divine grace and love.

Likewise, we can hold accountable the system and the people who killed him. They too are ends in themselves, and as such are responsible and accountable for their actions and decisions. When we understand humanity to be agents of reality, participators or co-creators in the world, then we are forced to reckon with the culpability that accompanies such actions. The presumption of freedom, autonomy, and subjectivity has led us to this affirmation of the agency and creativity of being human. It also leads us to understand the world and people within it as able to effect the destruction and violation of creation and community.

If we affirm with Kant that a human being is to be treated as an end rather than a means to another end, then we are able to understand the life of Jesus as valuable and important no matter the outcome. We are able to understand the death of Jesus as tragic and full of injustice, no matter the outcome. And we are able to celebrate the belief that God brings life out of death, creation out of chaos and destruction, no matter the final outcome.

Why Did He Die?

If we affirm and uplift the agency of human beings and apply it to this conversation about christology and atonement, we see how a change in theological anthropology entails a change in our thought about atonement and christology, and will eventually lead us to a proposal addressing a theology of the eucharist. The logic is this: what we understand about ourselves as human beings affects how we understand the humanity and the life of Jesus as Christ. Further: the way in which we understand Jesus as Christ affects what we will affirm about the sacraments, particularly the sacrament of the eucharist. The theologians that we have encountered through the course of this chapter have different proposals that get at these issues. For each of them, what is said about the human being in general is dramatized or exemplified in the understanding of Jesus, his life, and his relationship to the community and to God. Indeed that has been the direction of this project, in attempt to answer the fundamental questions about christology and atonement, first to explore and expand a notion of what it means to be human and to be in relationship to God, to examine the way in which traditional Christian communities have expressed this both in theology and in practice, and then to move toward what is perhaps the prime expression of an understanding of humanity in relationship to the divine—the sacraments.

It is clear, therefore, how the prior reconstruction of human agency feeds into an examination of what occurred in the events of Jesus' life and death. If we see that Jesus as a human being possessed an agency and a responsibility, we see that things were not merely done to him, he engaged the world and "stretched" it beyond itself. This is why he lived. The world responded in ways both loving and destructive. Rather than continue to be influenced by atonement theories that centralize and lead to a tacit approval of suffering and death, this proposal intends relies on some contemporary theological reflection allowing us to say that he died because they killed him—not because he deserved it, or because we deserve it, or even because God wanted it. He died because they killed him. Just as his agency brought him to this point, the agency of the persons who killed him brought them to their actions. He died because the dominant social order could not tolerate his ministry and his life, and he remained committed to it. We can mourn the death of Jesus, declare it tragic, and commit ourselves to working against the very powers which destroyed an attempt to bring about the vision of God.

We can also affirm that the role of God is not as the divine sanctioner of suffering, but as the one who works in the midst of suffering to bring about life, who refuses to allow tragedy to have the last word. This is stated not to dismiss or diminish in any way the charge of divine child abuse brought against Christian tradition and theology. If there is one thing that we ought not gloss over, dismiss, justify, or rationalize, it is the face that this charge is grounded in reality. It is only by taking the reality of violence in our society and our theology seriously that we can authentically construct an understanding of God that relates to humanity and the world in a compassionate and gracious manner.

This position is in line with much of the proposals from some of the theologians we have examined as they respond to the issues of atonement. However, the difference lies in the redefinition and emphasis on theological anthropology with resources in process thought and feminist theology as the means by which to answer the serious questions about christology and atonement. This proposal is more useful than those we have encountered, as it goes to what can be seen as the fundamental issue when speaking about Jesus' life and death: the relationship between God and the human being. As the basis for all that we affirm about Jesus, this relationship determines what Jesus does. As we have seen, if God is the dominating patriarch seeking restitution for an offense, the role of Jesus will be that of substitute, payment, sacrifice or satisfaction. If God is Sophia who lives in the midst of the human community, then Jesus is the one who embodied God's vision for the world.

The prior proposals from contemporary theologians enhance the notion that God's role in the world does not have to be conceptualized as abusive or controlling. There is a presumption about a definition of power in that argument. If we continue to understand God as wholly transcendent, omnipotent, and omniscient, then we have little means with which to understand the divine as mutually relational with the world—both affecting and being affected by the world.[60] But if we move in the direction that feminist theological principles and process theological construction urges us, we are enabled to understand God's power as reciprocal and fulfilled only through the relationship with the world. Whitehead's notion that God and the world, unity of vision and multiplicity of finites, seek completion/fulfillment in the other is a proposal that each finds its "heaven" in the other.

What do we take as resource to answer the question: Why did Jesus die? Williams' notion that Jesus did not come to be a surrogate is a strong point from which we can jump into a reformulation of understanding what he did come into the world to do. To shift the focus on the perceived point of Jesus away from his unfortunate death on the cross to the ministerial vision which he embodied insists that we value life, and that we find God working within the mission of human life, rather than requiring or accepting the need for sacrificial or substituted suffering and death. With Williams, we do not want to deny the reality of either the crucifixion of Jesus or the daily deaths suffered by multitudes of persons in the world, but we do want to understand what they mean for our lives.

Harrison also pushes us to reevaluate the virtue of sacrifice as it has been taught, embodied, and reinforced within Christian living and teaching. Suffering happens, death is a reality, violence remains a part of the world. The mission of Jesus put him in a position that led to his death. How we react to this speaks volumes about our theology. Do we gravely look upon the world as a place of risk, and faithfully choose our response to it? For some are more able than others—spiritually, physically, situationally—to take on the burdens of living in the vision of God. The gift of social power is not one to be taken lightly and enjoyed gluttonously. It is one to be tested and pushed within a world only too ready to challenge those who stand for justice, liberation and transformation.

---

[60] A fine reconstruction of God's power in this line of thought is found in Anna Case-Winters, *God's Power: Traditional Understandings and Contemporary Challenges* (Louisville: Westminster John Knox, 1990).

Suchocki's process/feminist reconstruction of the Christian idea of sin also pushes us to examine the reasons for the cross. To understand that sin is not a direct violation of God, but is a violation of the well-being of creation, locates human agency and culpability within the social realm. We sin against each other; We violate each other and the rest of the created world. God feels this as well. The suffering and death of Jesus was not a violation of God, it was a violation of the person that Jesus was; It was a violation of his personhood, his mission, and his community. Because of all of these things, it was therefore a violation of God. If we understand God as the giver of life and the sustainer of creation, continually working for and willing its well-being, then we can interpret the life of Jesus within that vision, as both incarnate model for human life and as gift of love from God for the world. God's presence as Jesus teaches the world, reveals the divine, touches human lives, and illumines a future. Jesus' death likewise teaches the world about itself, reveals the nature of the cosmos, touches human lives, and illumines the reality of evil.

The relationship determines the character of its participants, and the character of participants in a relationship determine the nature of their relationship. We have seen thus far in this book that God and the human being have been understood in varying ways throughout Christian theology. Whatever is said about one says something about the other, and what is said ultimately depends on or interprets what is said about the person and the role of Jesus as Christ in reconciling humanity with God. As we will see in our final chapter, what is said about the role of Jesus as Christ in this reconciling relationship affects sacramental theology. Jesus is institutor, presider, character and perhaps even substance of the sacraments, therefore we will move from our present understanding of christology and atonement into a sacramental theology.

We can see here how the particular proposals and their general themes aid us in answering the tough questions about Jesus' life and death, and about the relationship between God and humanity. Shifting our concept of God from one of static, transcendent, and demanding divinity to one of mutual, participatory, and engaging divinity goes with the proposal to understand the human being not merely as independent and self-sustaining rational being, but as a relational, responsible, and capable agent of reality. Each needs the other in order to reach a fuller version of itself—God and the world work in harmony, despite the dissonance that continues to resound throughout the cosmos.

The Mission of Jesus Is the Vision of God

One statement that has recurred in the latter portion of this chapter is this: The mission of Jesus is the vision of God. This comes most powerfully out of Delores William's analysis of atonement, and it has significance for our attempt to reframe the issues of christology and atonement. In Jesus' mission, i.e., his life and work, we discover what God's vision is. This is a vision for the world, an embodied hope for fulfillment and reconciliation. Within the context of her analysis, Williams spoke of the ministerial vision that Jesus brought about. The connection between the ministry that Jesus did, the activities in which he engaged, and the vision of God for right relations within the world, demonstrates the commitment of God to the world and to the covenantal relationship with humanity.

Jesus mission shows us the way of living envisioned by God for the purposes of transformation and radical love. God's vision is for the future of the world, a vision of reconciliation and justice. What Jesus did showed us what God wants and perhaps even what God hopes for the world. How he died showed God that the world still has its limits. Jesus' mission was to actualize the vision of God in the context of the world. The purpose for his very being was the do-ing. He did not live merely so that he could die. To say that about any human person limits the impact and value of their life both *coram mundo* and *coram Deo*. Jesus mission was to reveal God's vision, and along with doing that, his mission revealed the reality of the world. "At-one-ment" can thus be understood as the divine present with humanity, and the human reality unified with the divine vision. Reconciliation is for the broken and the violated world in need of healing and transformation. God acts in the midst of the violation to bring about new life. The mission of Jesus revealed that this is the vision of God.

5

Hoc est / Hoc facite:
Theology of the Eucharist as Indicative and Imperative

Review: Suggestion and Argument

WE come to the final portion of this journey of theological reflection on atonement and christology, the relationship between God and the human being, and the sacraments, to the portion where I cannot help but hear the echo of voices asking "so what?" Any good scholarly work ultimately asks and answers: So What? What does this material and your insight into it matter in the scheme of things? Can we learn anything, make anything better, make any difference for having gone through all of this? For that is the point of scholarship, if it is to have any purpose whatsoever, it ought to be that it gives us insight, that it equips us to do something in the world that matters, that makes life more sustainable for ourselves and for others. So what difference does it make to have addressed the issues of christology and atonement through a reexamination of the relationship between God and the human being?

It makes a difference in this way: Our participation in the eucharist signifies our embodied commitment to Jesus' mission, to the liberating vision of God. It signifies our willingness to risk for justice, to do whatever it takes, not regardless of, but despite the dangers involved. We are quite aware of and have deep regard for the dangers, for they can deter our commitment to bringing about the vision of God as Sophia/Wisdom. Through the eucharist as thanksgiving in community, we make a statement about this commitment and about the world, and we also celebrate the power of God to transform evil and suffering, to discover and develop potentiality in all things, and to create continuously. As creative agents, we make a conscious choice to participate actively in the world, and we have real ability to create, to effect change in the world. Guided by God as Sophia/Wisdom, human beings can act to bring about transformation in the world in accord with Her vision of truth, beauty, and goodness.

The chain of thought presented through this book is as follows: Atonement theories as they have been interpreted present troubling themes for understanding the human being and God in relationship. The trouble centers on Jesus' suffering and death presented as redemptive means to right relationship, and the understanding of God as completely powerful and the human being as passive and inept feeds into the problematic imagery. This book has shown that a return to the fundamental way in which we understand the relationship between God and the human being can help address some of these issues, and propose answers to some critical questions. In proposing some solutions, the book sparks a move to re-evaluate the way we understand the theology of the eucharist. The relationship between God and the human being is the basis from which we speak of christology and atonement, and our understanding of these things inevitably affects our understanding of the sacrament of eucharist.

In the course of this final chapter, I will revisit the concepts of the human being, God, and Jesus Christ to see how a reevaluation of them leads to implications for a theology of the eucharist. I will pay particular attention to what it means for human life to participate in the sacraments, and I will then emphasize five key themes which have arisen in this project that characterize a proposed theology of the eucharist.

The Human Being: Agent and Creative Participant

We have primarily relied upon feminist theological construction of a concept of the human being and of God, bringing in process thought with its philosophical resources and theological implications for speaking about experience and a concept of God. Each, in presenting an understanding of the world and of God, pushes us to reevaluate the way in which we view the world and God's relationship to it. These schools of thought share an emphasis on mutuality when speaking about the relationship between God and the human being. This is crucial to understanding the human being as agent and creative participant.

Mutuality relies upon the full participation of each party in a relationship, not independence and dependence respectively assigned. This understanding of mutuality is preferred over a presentation of the relationship between God and the human being which presents two characters existing on a spectrum of power and weakness, goodness and sinfulness. We saw this tendency in Luther's writings, as well as some theological reflection on the atonement. Mutuality more appropriately speaks to the human experience of the world which requires independence but relies on support from others—human and divine. Luther does offer some valuable insight into the relational dynamic between God and the human being but fails this proposal, however, when he dichotomizes the characters of God and the human being in terms of their power.

The feminist theological proposals in this book affirm the agency and ability of the human being to name her own reality and to engage in the ongoing work of transformation. The difference that this makes is that it preserves and encourages an understanding of all humanity as capable and responsible for life in this world. It does not shy away from but critically engages any presentation of humanity that presumes a passivity, an essential flaw that prevents such agency, or a fundamental inability or irrelevancy of human action. This comes directly out of feminist analysis of the human condition based on women's experience in the world. It does this in that feminist theology generally criticizes patriarchal cultural assumptions of female inferiority, and struggles to reclaim cultural value for women's voices and experiences.

Combining feminist theology with the other resources of this book, a constructive proposal for theological anthropology takes shape. As was shown, Luther's concept of the relationship between God and the human being is one centered on commitment and promise. The presence of God in the life of the human being is experienced physically in the practice of the sacraments of baptism and eucharist, and spiritually through covenant and faith; theological reflection on this emphasizes a commitment on the part of each. Luther's presentation of God is a God fully committed to be allied with the human in the presence of evil and suffering in the world. We can see how this image of God fits in with Ada Maria Isasi-Díaz's understanding of *la lucha*, and its role in human life. There is struggle, and God is present in the midst of it. It also ties in to Johnson's characterization of God as Sophia, present in and committed to the *Anfechtung* (Luther's term for personal struggles) of the world. In each case, struggle remains a fact in human life, and God remains committed to working through it with the human being. These emphases on struggle and commitment are two of the five themes in our final suggestions for a theology of the eucharist.

Luther also characterizes the human being enmeshed in the structures of the world, and he emphasizes that these structures of the world are not always in line with the vision of God. This speaks to the struggle that is human life, and this is one place at which Luther insists that humanity must depend on God for goodness, rely on grace for any ability to love and to better the world. The human being's activities in this world are addressed in an analysis of Luther's social ethics by George Forell. "This central importance of the relationship of God to man as established by the Gospel of the forgiveness of sins is the key to Luther's method."[1] It is important that here we understand Luther as speaking of the relationship of God to humanity. The relationship itself is the unidirectional work of God, and does not at all rely on the assent or action of the human being. The human being is in need of forgiveness from God, and God grants that forgiveness through grace. This relationship, therefore, becomes the basis from which the human being can and ought to live her life in accord with the divine will. The language of confrontation is used:

> Life confronts man with God, the creator God in the orders of nature established by Him to preserve the world, the saviour God in the Gospel of Christ which addresses man in the life-situation . . . . Social ethics is for Luther not the cause but the result of the confrontation of man by God.[2]

God comes to the human being, and the human being responds within the situation of life. Forell states that faith is active in love. It is clear that this understanding of humanity places the individual in the world which is a created place, an inferior location, but in relationship to God through God's own gracious will. At the same time, Luther maintains the connection between God and the human being, and the ineptitude of the human being on her own. The only way to speak of human life is *coram Deo*.

Doing good in the world, in relationship to the neighbor, flows from faith and a sense of Christian love. Forell allows us to connect this sense from Luther with our origins in the Kantian philosophical principles: "Luther considered love not a means to an end but the ethical end itself."[3] The human being is to love, and to act out of that love in and for the world, not in order to gain favor with God or to gain forgiveness, but because love is in itself an end. Beverly Harrison also emphasizes the importance of love as work, as acting-each-other-into-well-being, albeit in a different manner. The points where Luther fails lie in his concept of the human being who possesses a very limited sense of power. Particularly in relationship to God, the human being is utterly devoid of actual power. At the same time, we can see a vital connection between his insistence that love and acts of love toward the neighbor be considered ethical ends in themselves both to Kant's thought and to

---

[1] George W. Forell, *Faith Active in Love: An Investigation of the Principles Underlying Luther's Social Ethics* (New York: American, 1954) 64.

[2] Ibid., 68–69.

[3] Ibid., 102.

Harrison's urge that we love each other into well-being because God's vision for the well-being of the world depends upon it. It is not for some greater good or some transcendent purpose that we love and act within the world, it is for the here and the now, for the good of the world.

Working out of this synthesis of the anthropological concepts in Luther and contemporary theologies, we can affirm that the human being is intimately related to God, yet she remains distinctive and independent in her humanity. The balanced tension between relation and individual agency for God and the human being remains crucial, emphasizing mutuality, but characterizing a fine line which must be tread. The human being is herself an agent, capable of effecting real transformation in the world, yet still guided and sustained by God, who is connected to and still more than her and the world. God is intimately a part of the world as a whole, yet transcends the world as divine agent, allowing the wisdom of divine guidance to take shape.

It is agency on which this proposal for thinking about the human being turns. It is a concept which is largely absent from Luther, in terms of the human being's individual character in relationship with God. In his sacramental writings, it was theologically and ecclesial-politically necessary to remove efficacy from human activity: theologically so because Luther knew that he could never be sure of the sufficiency of his own actions as a sinner in order to be justified, and ecclesial-politically so because Luther sought to correct the Roman church as they tried to wrest control of the efficacy of the eucharist from God to serve their own interests. While the context of these sacramental debates determines Luther's understanding of human effective activity in the sacraments, in terms of bringing about the connection to God, I believe that it is a larger theme for Luther's theology and his concept of the human being. God works in us and we respond through faith. Luther is bound in some manner to his own era. Taking into account feminist criticism of his theological theme about what it means to be human, it is appropriate to depend more fully on a contemporary theological analysis of the human condition in relationship to God while retaining the dynamic of the relationship between God and the human being we find in Luther. His powerful theocentrism pulls contemporary theology back toward the relationship as it attempts to define humanity.

In feminist and in process theologies, experience is the core of construction, both of the world in its many members, and of the self. The human being is not only subject of her own moral law- and decision-making capacity, *auto nomos*, she is an agent in her own life, acting out of that subjective experience in tandem with God. With Luther, this proposal seeks to emphasize the alliance of God with humanity. I would like to say that this is a choice on the part of each, but I feel compelled to say that it is in the nature of each to be in this mutually enhancing relationship. In any case, God and the human being engage in *la lucha* together, each bringing her own character strengths and flaws to the table, and both renewing a commitment daily to the struggle, refusing to allow the struggle or suffering to define her life and her relationships.

When we understand the human being as agent and creative participant in the world and in the relationship with God, we understand her participation in the eucharist as an intentional and creative activity, signifying her commitment to God, as seen in the life and mission of Jesus. We understand her participation as freely chosen and full of intentionality. This intentionality is tied to an understanding of Jesus' person and mission, which we will review after explicating our present comprehension of God.

God: Visioner and Sustainer

As it is difficult to speak of the human being without speaking of God, the reverse is true. The separation of the two characters may be an artificial one, if we are to insist that human life is *coram Deo*. However, relationships presume two participants who have their own identity at some level, and it is our task here to discern the identities of God and the human being and the ways in which they play into the dynamic of relationality.

> We advocate, then, that the triune nature of God be expressed directly through the understanding of God's presence with us and for us through Jesus of Nazareth, through the wisdom of God whereby God brings the church to birth in each generation, guiding it through divine providence in its manifestation of apostolicity, unity, and holiness, and through the power of God, bringing the world to justice within the transformation of the divine nature and guiding the world toward societal forms of justice.[4]

God has already been discussed extensively as the one who is ultimately committed to the human being and the world. This is the presence of the divine who is "with us and for us," experienced through the person of Jesus. God has also been named as Sophia/Wisdom, the one who brings the world and the church into fuller realizations of itself, guiding and sustaining the processes of life. This project has been undergirded and guided by an eye toward general issues of justice like liberation and transformation. Marjorie Suchocki's statement above packs all of these things into a lively affirmation of the triune nature of a God who is with us (present) and for us (advocate)

---

[4] Marjorie Hewitt Suchocki, *God–Christ–Church: A Practical Guide to Process Theology* (New York: Crossroad: 1982, 1989) 234.

bodily (Jesus) and spiritually (lure). All of these are essential to that which we are developing here.

In Whitehead's terms, God can be understood as the fellow-sufferer who understands, while still being the one who acts as the poet of the world, leading it toward harmony. Luther insists that God relates to the world through covenant, and that the relationship therefore is one that is covenantal, infusing the human being with meaning and significance far beyond herself. This intentional aspect of the divine relationship with the human being is one that makes a difference for Luther on the part of God, and for us here it ought to make a difference on the part of the human being. What if the human being, through her faith and concrete expressions of that faith, is being intentional about her relationship with God, not merely allowing herself to be acted upon, but receiving the gifts given her *in order to* act in the world for the vision of God?

We cannot be intentional about some matters in our lives: our physical make-up, our social location, our personality. However, we can be intentional about how we respond to those things which make up our lives. What do I do with the fact that I have the gift of comfortable social position? What do I do with the fact that I am female in a patriarchal world? What difference does my white skin make in a racist culture? The difference that agency makes is that it allows the individual to respond actively out of her particular situation. In this way, no person is fully determined by that which is given to or taken from her. We can see the influence of a Whiteheadian metaphysic on this statement: no moment of concrescence is fully determined by that which came before it; the elements of freedom, novelty, and creative synthesis remain crucial parts of the process of becoming. This includes the human being working with or against the vision of God.

Luther, of course, was wary of any and all attempts to maintain human ability to do anything that directly affects the relationship with God. Justification occurs not through any merit on the part of the person, but by the grace of God, through our faith in Christ. God is the giver, both of life and of vision. If we affirm that God is committed to the human being and to the world, we can move away from the imagery and language of judgment or ruling to the process theological influenced notion of the vision of God. The vision is that which God lures the world toward, that which consists of the fullest expression of all forms of life. Vision is another of the themes which will be lifted up at the end of this chapter.

Delores Williams spoke of the ministerial vision which Jesus enacted through his life and ministry. We will return to the ministry aspect of this proposal in the following section, but it is important to clarify briefly what the vision of God can mean. It is not as if God actually sees (visions) what the future will be; It is as if God en-visions what the future can be, and acts in the present moments of the world to bring each individual life the chance to become closer to that possibility. "A vision" does not act as functional ideals to which we must assent, rather it functions "as-if." We ought to live "as-if" we are in the sight/vision of God. We ought to act and live in community "as-if" justice for all were attainable. The element of faith is present in all of these things. Implied here is the often harsh reality that there is rarely any agreement on a common good, on the existence of God, on the actual possibility of justice. Whatever form the details take, living and acting "as-if" does not deny the sometimes harsh reality, in fact it engages reality for the purposes of transformation, implying that there is hope, there is a vision of something better and greater and deeper and fuller that we locate with God.

To speak of human life *coram Deo* has these meanings, insisting that we understand both what it means to be in the presence of God, and to live responsibly in actualizing the vision of God. Our human subjectivity must move us toward realizing our human agency. God as Sophia is this sort of divine visioner, the sustainer of life and hope and justice. It is this divine presence which "should not be spoken about in terms of a suffocating, overwhelming shadow but rather as the ground of freedom itself."[5] The power of God is not controlling and does not determine all things in the world. Rather, understood in our language of mutuality, it is an empowering power: "The glory of God is being manifest to the degree that creatures are most radically and fully themselves."[6] If we engage the concept of God as Sophia, and we embrace the concept of the vision of God, we will be able to see how the sacraments as physical manifestation of the relationship between God and the human being must also be engaged. We move from the image of a God who demands, allows, or controls the events surrounding the life and death of Jesus, to a God who continually works within the world and with humanity to create a reality closer to a fuller expression of the future envisioned by God. This move insists that we understand the sacraments not only as gifts, as infusers of faith, as actions of God, but also as symbolic of our participation with God in the actualization of a vision, and our expression of commitment to the vision of God. This is what we first saw in the ministry of Jesus.

Jesus Christ: Person and Mission

There is a problem of the eucharist which lies in its connection to sacrificial or substitutionary or any other theoretical atonement implications. The re-

---

[5] Elizabeth A. Johnson. *She Who Is: The Mystery of God in Feminist Theological Discourse* (New York: Crossroad, 1992) 229.

[6] Ibid.

construction of our understanding of the life, death, and resurrection of Jesus ultimately enables us to return to the problem with adequate answers. The reconstruction of the relationship between God and the human being allows us to do this. The Christ event presumes and communicates an understanding of God's relationship with the human being. Through a renewed understanding of the relationship, we can express a transformed understanding of the event, and subsequently the practice of the eucharist as the ritual embodying that very connection.

With Philip Hefner, we can say that Jesus is a paradigm of God and the human being working intimately to bring about a vision of truth, beauty, and goodness. Likewise, Gerd Theissen says about Jesus, "He is the image of God, what man should be."[7] We ought to see a connection between "being" and "doing," for ourselves and for our relationship with God. As Harrison affirms, Jesus was the social radical, the prophet who himself embodied God in the world. Because of this embodiment, Jesus' ministry on behalf of the poor and disenfranchised peoples put him in conflict with the moral and social order of his time. He made choices which entailed some particular possibilities of risk. The path of his life opened up certain sets of possibilities, and one of those possibilities included death.

This element of risk is one that is crucial to the final proposal of this project. Life in the world entails risk, due to the finite and fragile nature of things and of societies. Bodies break, lives end, and societies can destroy. Human life is always fragile, and if it is lived *coram Deo*, it becomes all the more risky. This is not because the world and God are opposed to one another, rather that the world is not yet fully in line with God's vision for the future. God continues to work in the world, to create within the world. If we speak of evil in this project, we speak of it in terms of the structures of reality that entail tragedy in their very nature. Darby Ray proposes that we think of the atonement as the theological doctrine which enables us to speak of God's confrontation with evil in the world. It becomes the means by which we speak of a human and divine response to the presence of tragedy.

We can say that Jesus was a prophet, one who worked in order to bring about transformation in the community, in individual lives, and in the world. This is the embodiment of alliance with God. The statement from an earlier chapter returns: The mission of Jesus is the vision of God. Building upon our notion of the vision of God as that lure and drive toward fuller realization of life, we can say that Jesus' mission was to actualize that vision in the midst of community. He taught, ministered, preached, and lived "as-if" the vision

---

[7] Gerd Theissen, *Biblical Faith: An Evolutionary Approach,* trans. John Bowden (Philadelphia: Fortress, 1984) 106.

of God were being fulfilled, "as-if" the kingdom were at hand. His work brought the world closer to the reality of God, to its own potential, and to the implications of the relationship between the two. We can "see" the vision of God personified in the mission of Jesus.

God continuously creates and humans continually participate in the transformation that is creation. Jesus was a part of this transformation as he was driven toward attaining aesthetic and creative worth for members of the community as a part of the vision of God. On the basis of this drive, he engaged in activities that were risky, that put him in conflict with the political power structures of his time. He was in conflict with God about these choices as well, pleading that the risks not continue to be so great. "Again he went away for the second time and prayed, 'My Father, if this cannot pass unless I drink it, your will be done'" (Matthew 26:42). And he prayed a third time, but became a victim of the fact that the will of God is enmeshed in the power structures of the world, affected by the decisions and the actions of human beings.

What if the Christian Holy Week centered not around the dark veiling of the cross on Friday and the bright white Easter lilies on Sunday, but around the "Thursday night" struggle? The decision was his to make. The commitment had been made, so the decision became clear. Because Jesus was committed to the vision of God, he committed his life to a course of events that led to the cross. The supper, the gathered community, the service to one another, the betrayal and the risk which was Jesus' life ought to inform Christian tradition and practice in a more meaningful manner, as they highlight the very things that we have examined in this project. If we take freedom seriously, then we have to take seriously the possibility that Jesus could have fled. He did not, and the consequences were tragic. God did not abandon the process either, and through the resurrection, we can see God working within the limits of the world to actualize a fuller realization of life.

The power of evil present in the system and persons within it brought about destruction upon Jesus and his ministry. It was ultimately because of his ministry that he was killed. We may assert that Jesus did not die because we did something wrong, or because he did something wrong, he died because they killed him. If we take seriously the insistence that human beings are responsible for their own actions in this world, as agents of their own lives, we must hold accountable the people and the power structures that demanded his death. If we also take seriously a concept of God who works with but does not control the world, we can affirm divine goodness and grace as that which works out of the decisions of the world for transformation and new life. As Jesus suffered, God suffered, and God is the one who is able to work in the midst of the struggle, the pain and the death in order to bring the human community back to faith in life again.

What, then, do we do with the entire idea of a sacrificial or substitutionary or ransom or any theory of atonement (at-one-ment) which centers on the suffering and death of Jesus as the means for reconciliation? In this series of events, God and the world are brought into right relationship with one another, presuming some sort of previous violation of that relationship. Asserting that the "right" relationship between God and humanity was achieved through the crucifixion and resurrection entails the risk of necessitating or sanctioning the suffering and death of Jesus. It does this because it goes beyond acknowledging the fact that struggle, even suffering, exists in human life. Atonement theory traditionally maintains that suffering is the *means* by which salvation, or right-relationship with God, is brought about. This is the point that this study is attempting to change.

Relying on a Kantian drive to treat things as ends in themselves partly helps resolve this tension. As an end itself, Jesus' life provided a glimpse of what God envisions for the world. As an end itself, Jesus' death was tragic. As an end itself, the resurrection is the Christian celebration of God's ability to work in the midst of even death. The relationship between God and the human being is dramatically embodied in these moments. We maintain a protest stance toward these events of suffering and bloodshed: It ought not happen this way. We find God in the midst of them as the one who envisions a better reality, and who sustains hope in the present reality through continual creation with the cooperation of humanity.

We can describe the activity of God as fundamentally the activity of creative transformation. Although God could not systematically alter the power structures of injustice that carried out the death of Jesus, God worked in the midst of that evil to bring about transformed life, and an understanding in the community that She never abandons the world. "In the midst of the isolation of suffering the presence of divine compassion as companion to the pain transforms suffering, not mitigating its evil but bringing an inexplicable consolation and comfort."[8] Consolation, comfort and transformation come from God to the human being. This can only come through an intimate and committed presence of the divine in the world. What does this evaluation of Jesus' person and mission, in light of what we are saying about the relationship between God and the human being, imply for a discussion of the sacraments?

---

[8] Johnson, *She Who Is*, 267.

Participation in the Sacraments: Eucharist and Human Life

Five key words have become thematic for this discussion of the relationship between God and the human being, manifest in Jesus as Christ, and expressed through the sacraments: *Commitment, mission, vision, risk*, and *struggle*. I will now take each of these terms and look at its implications for speaking specifically about participation in the sacraments. In our exploration of the sacraments, I included Luther's writings on both baptism and eucharist. This was done intentionally as there are thematic elements present in his "sacramental theology" in general that are best demonstrated by analysis of his writings on both sacraments. For purposes of the final portion of this book, I am going to limit the discussion to participation in the eucharist.

The eucharist is that sacrament which is most obviously and directly connected to the contentious elements that we have explored through this book: the death of Jesus—its meaning, God's presence, and human response. Indeed, when I began germinating the seeds of this project in my mind, I started thinking about the cross, the theology of the cross and some feminist theological responses to it. Through a series of conversations, I realized that what really made these matters important to me was what they said about God and the human being and their relationship, and the way in which this is all expressed through the eucharist. I further determined that to look at the sacrament of holy communion in Luther would be incomplete unless one looked at the larger issues in his theology that are expressed in his writings on the sacraments: the cycle of death and rebirth, the need for humiliation for exaltation, the power of sign, significance, and faith, and the role of God and the human being throughout all of these things. We will now see how five words suggestively inform this theological reflection on our participation in the eucharist.

Commitment

God is committed to the world; humanity is committed to the vision of God. Both of these statements find public sacramental expression in the eucharist. God's commitment to the world is such that the divine became incarnate in the world, to embody the vision through a mission of justice and liberation. This commitment involves the vision that God has for the world, and it is felt in the daily ways in which God sustains humanity. God as Sophia brings both the wisdom and the commitment to emancipation that are required for a viable future.

Through participation in the eucharist, the human being publicly signifies her commitment to the vision of God, and stands in *communio, coram Deo*. Living a life in relationship to God begins in her baptism when God makes that commitment, and her relationship with God moves through ups and downs as any relationship will—at times feeling more intimate, at time incredibly distant. The eucharist is a reminder to herself and to the community gathered that she remains committed, despite the temptations to find fulfillment elsewhere. It is the expression of her commitment to the life which Jesus lived, and her acknowledgement of the utter injustice surrounding the circumstances of his death.

Commitment is difficult, and commitment involves risk, which we will examine in itself. When one is committed to something or someone, part of that person is bound in some manner to the well-being of the other. Commitment must remain a freely chosen and intentional activity on the part of both God and the human being. At the same time, it is within the very nature of each character to be in such a covenantal relationship. To invest worth in the other as an extension of the self can be expressed both as a dynamic between the divine and the human, and as a dynamic between humans. The risk element comes in when we accept the vulnerabilities involved in relationship.

Mission

Jesus' mission is God's vision. This statement appears again because it succinctly provides a connection between the rather abstract notion of the vision of God and the reality of Jesus' life in the world, his ministry to and for peoples in need, in contradiction to the power structures of his time. The mission is the concrete reality of how God's vision can play out in this world. The mission reveals something about the world, and something about God. It reveals that God supports the underside of human community—those persons who are despised and reviled for their station in life. It reveals that God works for the causes of justice and liberation, and therefore that these are components of the vision of God.

Jesus' mission further reveals things about the world. It reveals that the world cannot withstand the full power of God's vision. It reveals that the world is not always in accord with God, indeed that it attempts to destroy the actuality of God whenever it can. Evil is real in the world, and God must confront it through the eyes and the lives of the believers. The mission reveals also that the world is a place of great potential, and that tremendous creative possibility exists for goodness and beauty. Humanity can be a part of both sides of this revelation about the world—either as destructive obstacles, or as creative participants.

The fact that the mission of Jesus ended as it did brings us to the sacramental meal in which we continue to participate. What does the meal accomplish as far as Jesus is concerned? It brings the community together on the eve of and in the face of tremendous risk and potential destruction. It expresses Jesus' commitment to the community, his commitment to the vision of God, and God's commitment to the world. It insists on remembrance and participation—doing this with the mission in mind. To have the mission in mind is to commit oneself to it, to work in the context of one's own life to actualize a bit of the vision of God.

Vision

We have spoken extensively about the vision of God. What does it mean to have vision? Either to see or to envision is to have some capacity for comprehending the world. To see something is to take it into one's being. One theological proposal contends that to see certain things is to know a deeper level of reality, and to know that reality is to become involved in it. "Compelling knowledge" is that knowledge which compels the knower/seer to *do* something in response. It starts with the eyes and the head, the seeing and the knowing; it moves to the heart and the commitment; and it comes to completion in the hands and the action taken.[9] Further, as we have seen in discussing the term "*coram*," to see something is to be in relationship to it, to have one's face turned toward it.

Vision of God: sight of God or plan of God? When taken as a metaphor to speak about the human being's relationship to God, these images connote powerful things. One meaning of the Latin word, *coram*, is "before the eyes of," or to be in the sight of another. When, with Luther, we speak of the human being *coram Deo*, we speak of the human being in direct relationship with God, in the presence of God, and being attended to by God. We have insisted that the person be known as an agent, that she not be presented as passive object of a gaze, but as active participant in taking in and acting out from those things around her. The vision of God, when vision is understood as the dream, hopes, or envisioned plan of God for the future, becomes that which the human being can discern and actualize. When the human being lives a life *in* the vision of God, she also lives *for* the vision of God. If God's presence is both with and for the human being, then the human being is present both with and for God.

The important implication of the term vision is, of course, to envision something. We have spoken of God's vision for the world, and this requires not only relationship to the world, but commitment to its improvement and capacity to think beyond its present state. This is laced with hope while be-

[9] This comes from and is explicated creatively by Mary Solberg in *Compelling Knowledge: A Feminist Proposal for an Epistemology of the Cross* (New York: SUNY Press, 1997).

ing tinged with harsh reality and implies that God's creative transformation moves out of the particularity of the world to incorporate it into the principles of truth, beauty, and goodness. When something is envisioned, it is not clearly seen. There is a sort of haze around it, and the particulars may not be exactly known. The shape may be understood, or the sense of things, but not the precise way in which it Is because it is not yet determined. This is important, as it shows us how God does not "see" the future, but can envision it and have some sense of what can become out of that which is the world. This vision is brought into reality only through the actual lives and work in the world. Its precise form is thus determined by the actions in the world, and another vision begins to take shape out of that reality. Participation in the eucharist is one part of our living in the vision.

This sense of the word "vision" depends upon our process theological understanding of God's relationship with the world. God is not the one who sees the future clearly as it is predestined to be. Rather, life is a continual process, once which God participates in as the lure toward this vision. God envisions the best possibility for any given moment. Whitehead spoke of the aesthetic principles of truth, beauty, and goodness. As a part of God's vision, these things guide humanity toward a fuller expression of life, and a more creative response to matters in the world. As a process, life is continually being actualized, and God's vision continually responds to the actuality in ways that emphasize the potential for truth, beauty, and goodness. When the world fulfills its potential as envisioned by God, then it moves further into the vision of God.

Vision belongs not solely to God. If human beings are created in the image of God, then they possess some of this capacity to envision and to create anew. The very suggestion of freedom implies this capacity to do not solely as has been determined, but to have the ability to choose freely between options and among creative syntheses of options. The hopeful element of this is that humanity can and will choose the good, or at least the best possibility. However, the human capacity for choice and creative synthesis involves the ability to synthesize elements of the world in such a way as to move farther from God, to bring harm and ill-being on the world and the self. God works even in these moments, and continually presents the lure toward actualizing the vision.

In the moments of the eucharist, the human being renews her commitment and to the vision that God made real in the person of Jesus. Doing this in remembrance of him who lived out the vision of God signifies that the human being continues to believe in the power of the divine vision to overcome the stark reality that is often the world. It is a simultaneous acknowledgement of the tragic and the triumphant, and it is a moment of engagement between God and the human being.

Risk

The final two components of this argument are those which speak most directly to the presence of evil in the world. We have not spent a great deal of time explicating a theodicy in this project, although it underlies certain aspects of the argument. Evil is taken as a given, as a part of the world which is not in accord with the vision of God, which worked to impede its actualization. We have not and will not here address the question Whence evil? but will simply accept the reality of it. The questions of its origins are seeds for another project altogether. Evil makes the world a place of risk, and it made Jesus' mission a risky venture. Our participation in the eucharist signifies our willingness to risk for justice, to bring about the vision of God despite the dangers involved.

To speak of danger is to speak of evil, and to speak of evil is to speak of the world as it is separated from God. It is that aspect of the world which God does not, and can not control. There is this inherent risk in freedom, the risk that the choice will be made not to assent to the lure of God, to deny one's potential for good, and choose violence and violation. Since this is a real possibility, the world is characterized in part by risk; there is a risk which threatens well-being, the search for justice, and the struggle for liberation. Human life is characterized by the struggle that we will explicate in the next section. The sense of struggle has roots in this understanding of risk within the context of the world.

Jesus expressed a willingness to take the risk, and we express our willingness in the eucharist, as he commanded, "do this in remembrance of me." Awareness of the dangers involved in such commitment serves the individual as she prepares to deal with whatever the world throws her way. If we do not know that there is risk involved in leading a faithful life, then we do not know what it means to live a faithful life. A person living a faithful life seeks to actualize the fullness of the vision of God, and he or she is characterized by creative agency, commitment to, and relationship with God. Ideally, the faithful individual lives in community and acts in the world according to her will, in accord with the vision of God. She is capable, responsible, and hopeful.

To be capable and responsible means that the individual accepts the consequences of her actions, knows that her actions may be met with opposition, and works so that her community may see the grace of God. Her participation in the eucharist is her public acknowledgement of God' presence in her life and the world, of the risks involved in living this faithful life, and her commitment to continuing the mission that was begun in Jesus. She shares with the community her fear and anger and uncertainty, and shares with the community in the gifts of God, the vision and the sustenance needed to attain the vision.

Participation is risk, it is activity which acknowledges that a life lived fully in the presence of God, *coram Deo*, in the vision/sight of God, for the vision/plan of God, entails conflict with structural evils, and potential for ultimate transformation, from death to life, from absence to presence, and from despair to hope. This participation involves the risk and commitment illustrated by the paradigm of Jesus as Christ. Participation in the eucharist, therefore, allows the individual to step up and renew the commitment, and publicly stand with the community in defiance of the system of destruction which brought about this meal in the first place.

Struggle

The words for struggle have come to this project from two diverse sources: Luther's concept of *Anfechtung*, and Isasi-Díaz's use of *la lucha*. Each uses the word to signify the inherent nature of struggle in human life, and the places in which human beings find ultimate comfort and consolation in God. For Luther, *Anfechtung* is tied to the assailing forces of the world which tempt the human being to sin, and cause him to despair and even lose trust in God. It represents the internal struggle of discerning worthiness in the presence of God. For Isasi-Díaz, *la lucha* is a fact of human life, particularly as she sees it in Hispanic women's lives: The fact that women struggle for daily sustenance and survival. For both, the struggle is a part of living in the world, and it is where God can be seen working with the human being both to comfort and to give strength. Isasi-Díaz explicitly states that this is the context out of which Hispanic women can name and gain their strength, to celebrate survival, and to rejoice in moving from day to day.

Struggle indicates relationality in many different ways. In struggle, there can be opposing forces: good and evil, justice and destruction, liberation and enslavement, or any combination of these. In struggle, there can also be multitudes of competing interests, and this can take shape in many different ways: the human interest in preserving well-being and the human drive to protect oneself and one's loved ones often come into conflict. This could be seen in an act of self-defense, or in an act of life sustenance. One could kill another to protect one's child, and one could kill an animal to feed one's child. Weighing the competing interests and drives in human life itself is a struggle.

Relationality within struggle as we have been discussing it here also involves the relationship of God with the world, and of God with the human being. Luther's theology of the cross locates God in the midst of the struggle that is the cross. The competing forces and conflicting interests of that event culminated in the death of the man who sought to share the word of God with the community. His attempts to bring the community to a closer realization of God, to a fuller expression of themselves, were brought to an end by the forces and interests which felt threatened. This particular struggle between God and the world was "won" in the cross by the world. As we know, that was not the last chapter of the struggle, and God continued to work in the world to bring new life and new realization of the divine vision to expression through the communities of believers.

An important dimension of this is the presence of God in the struggle. Jesus was not, and we are not, left alone to fend against evil or to discern the conflicting interests of life in the world. God's commitment means that God is present, and God's covenant ensures that such presence is unfailing. One of the struggles which is also one of the gifts of human life is that not only do we live *coram Deo*, we live *coram mundo* and *coram hominibus*. We have the community around us at any given time, and when we recognize it and participate in it we share both burdens and joys, as Luther counseled so many centuries ago. The sacrament of the eucharist gives us this opportunity, to hear the word and to actively respond in renewing our commitments to God and the world.

Hoc est / Hoc facite: The Indicative and Imperative

A theological statement about the eucharist must finally say that the indicative and imperative elements of the sacrament must be conjoined. The eucharist makes a statement about the world, and it makes a statement about what the world ought to be. The world is a place where bodies are broken and blood is shed. The indicative is tragic. The indicative is also hopeful: The world is also a place where we are connected in community and in remembrance and in covenant to God and to those who came before us. We are to remember this, and act in the world "as-if" the vision of God were a reality. The imperative is hopeful and it is a call to action. It presumes something about the human being, that he or she is capable and responsible, and it presumes something about the relationship of God to the human life, that the relationship is committed and intimate and difficult.

We cannot fully appreciate the imperative without the indicative, and we cannot live in the indicative without the imperative. To remain mired in the tragic structures of the world would entail losing hope and trust in God. To get "stuck" in the cross as the definitive moment for Christian theology is to imply troubling and destructive things about God. We need the theological ability to both take this seriously and to carefully and creatively move out of that, always remembering but not being defined by it. Likewise, we cannot simply celebrate the joys of new life and the beauty of a sunny Easter morning without knowing that the world was, is, and will in some ways continue to be a troubling and destructive place. We need the theological ability to celebrate this while remaining grounded in the reality of the world and the continued need for transformation in our lives and in the lives of those around us.

The eucharist gives us opportunity to do these things, theologically and practically. It is that moment in the life of the Christian church which blends tragedy and celebration like no other. This has indeed been a source of problems, when the tragedy is celebrated, or the celebration is dampened by the deep sense of the tragic. Rather than fall to either of these extremes, the proposal here is that we engage both seriously, as ends in themselves, as characteristics of the world in which we live.

We ought to be thankful for the community gathered around us. We ought to celebrate the presence of God in the face of the one next to us. As we participate in the meal, we participate in the life of the church in its deepest expression. This is my body, broken for you . . . . This is my blood, shed for you. It is not because of you that I was killed, it was for the sake of life in the vision of God, in which you now have opportunity to participate. But you know, as we all must, that people are still being killed for their ministry, being silenced for their message, and being destroyed for their relationships. This is wrong. You will do this in remembrance of me, and in remembrance of all those who have suffered, who do suffer, and who will continue to suffer. You will remember that as a part of this mission, and you now live a life of risk. Your commitment to this is a gift of God in itself, and God will be with you through the darkest and the brightest moments of your life. You know that there is more, there is something better, and you have the ability to work with God to bring that vision to actuality.

The sacrament of the eucharist can be understood in this way: It is an expression of Christian faith, and a participation in the vision of God. When Jesus said do this, what was he asking of us? Do this: live like this, commit yourself to this, remember this is the way: This is the vision of God, of a world embodying mutuality and justice, truth, beauty, and goodness. Do these things in remembrance of those who have come before and have suffered because of their commitments. This is what we affirm when we "do this in remembrance of me." Our participation in this ritual becomes one of giving thanks to God for alliance, for the strength to continue.

6
Conclusion

Human beings fundamentally live their lives *coram Deo*. To live life *coram Deo* means that the individual is in community with other persons and with God. It brings us to the table and the font, and hopefully it brings us to fuller realization of ourselves and our future as a world. In the spirit of optimism, we affirm that God's vision for the future is something in which we participate, in which we can make a difference for the good, and in which we find ourselves whether or not we comprehend the significance of it. In the presence of tragedy, we affirm that God's presence makes a difference for the survival of the human community, and that it enables creative responses that attempt to derive meaning from life in the world.

Underlying the journey of this project is an acknowledgement of the reality of evil and its power to distract and dissuade the world from living fully within the vision of God. Unfortunately, to my way of thinking it is a "given" in any reflection on human life, and on the ways in which humanity does or does not quite fulfill its potential to live a co-creative agents with God. Rather than deal directly with the problem of evil, I have chosen through the course of this book to deal with the ways in which humanity can, does, and ought to work with the problem of good, the burden of potential, and the responsibility of agency. If we affirm that we can make a difference, than we have the responsibility to make that difference in the world.

While these larger concerns and questions have guided this project, it is the specific problems of violence and suffering as a part of the Christian atonement story that have directed the constructive proposals. In fact, these reflections have been as much of a personal journey toward answers as it has been a scholarly exercise. Upon confronting the sharp criticisms and questions found in some feminist theologies, we must wrestle with the issues raised, and take seriously the ways in which experience of Christian doctrine and/or practice has been divisive and destructive to spirits and bodies. This is one of those responsibilities for a person living in the vision of God. The vision for a future is coupled with the vision that sees what has happened in our past and is happening in our presence. Accountability demands that we see where and what we have been as a Christian community, and that we use our cognitive gifts to mark out our direction for a future in relationship with God.

The problem with which we have been directly concerned to answer is the charge that Christianity is an abusive theology that glorifies suffering. Throughout the course of this study I have suggested that reevaluating the relationship between God and the human being enables us to address this charge. The answer therefore is this: If we understand God to be the visioner and sustainer of life, and if we understand the human being to be an agent and creative participant in the work of the world, then we can recognize that the death of Jesus on the cross was not willed or intended by God. If we understand that God's power does not entail an ability to control all things, and that human beings can make choices that are not in accord with the vision of God for the world, then we can recognize that Jesus died on the cross because the power structures of his time could not withstand the message of radical good news. We can further recognize that God is the one who works in the midst of the world and continually creates it anew and brought about the new life which Christians celebrate through the resurrection. The sacrament of the eucharist is the expression of these things and is the public reminder that the work of love is not yet complete.

At the end of this study, it is clear that there are as many unresolved issues as there may be proposals for rethinking Christian theology. Some of those issues will be mentioned here, not in attempt to resolve them, but in hopes that future scholarship, my own or that of someone else, will take up the serious challenges of doing theology in the contemporary world.

Ethics

This book has been mainly concerned with the theological ways we understand the relationship between God and the human being for purposes of addressing some critical issues in atonement theories and leading to a renewed vision of the eucharist. Any conversation about human life in the world, however, is incomplete without reflection on ethics. To take seriously what it means to be human means that we must engage in ethical reflection. This book has spoken generally about working in the world to actualize the vision of God. The ethicist could ask, "What does this look like? How does it work?"

> The particular cries, social forces, and relationships affecting human beings evoke the ethical questions that matter to people. This is where a pastorally engaged ethical method begins. The heart of what we as Christians profess is that God became incarnate not in an abstract sense but in the historical particularities of Jesus of Nazareth.[1]

If we are going to seriously engage a shift from speaking of human beings as subjects to speaking of persons as agents, then we lead directly into an ethical conversation. Living in the world is a real thing and has real consequences, and the Christian community deserves an adequate ethical framework for understanding this. It is my hope that the theological concepts explored in this study provide some impetus for further ethical reflection on human life in the vision of God. What *does* it mean?

Theological anthropology as such is incomplete without ethics. Likewise, theological ethics depends upon a conversation that asks the very basic questions of what it means to be human, particularly in relationship with God. That is the fundamental question of this project, and the answers proposed herein may lead us to some conversation about the implied ethics in its understanding of being human *coram mundo* and *coram Deo*. Morality and justice are related topics within this discussion, and both merit further examination in future projects.

Theodicy

Throughout this book, reference has been made to the underlying and assumed presence of evil in the world. It presumes a protest stance toward evil as the tragic character of the world. It is simply wrong that persons must suffer needlessly and that justice does not always prevail. The study has not, however, addressed the crucial question of "whence evil?". From where does evil come? This affects our very concept of God—because if we affirm that God is the creator of all things, then God can be posited as the author of evil.

The traditional problem of theodicy is one that continues to provoke thoughts about God and the world: If God is all-powerful and all-benevolent, from where does evil come? In discussing this classic conundrum, theologians generally are seen to "compromise" or redefine one aspect of the question. Perhaps one redefines God's power, as in the process theologian Charles Hartshorne, or one clarifies God's goodness. Maybe one can even classify the reality of evil as an illusion or a misperception on the part of limited human ability to grasp God's greater purposes. Any way that one approaches

---

[1] Karen Bloomquist, "In Today's Context," in *The Promise of Lutheran Ethics*, ed. Karen L. Bloomquist and John R. Stumme (Minneapolis: Fortress, 1998) 6.

the question of God's justice with regard to the reality of evil, the answers do not come easily. There is no agreement on how to perceive God's role in the world, and thus there is no all-encompassing answer to the problem of theodicy.

It is my hope that this study has been honest about the simple reality of evil. I believe that this is one thing that ought not be disputed. Evil is real. While maintaining a genuine optimism about the ability of God and the human being to work together to bring about a greater world, a fuller reality, and a better future, the theological proposals engaged and offered in this project never lose sight of the injustice and violation that is a part of human life in the world. While saying that nothing can justify the death of the man Jesus on the cross, we have sought to understand how God is present in the midst of the suffering and works in the middle of our struggles to actualize a better reality.

The questions of theodicy will never be fully answered to the satisfaction of all. It is my hope that the reflections offered here aid the conversation in a constructive manner. I trust that more work is yet to be done on theodicy, and I think that understanding the role of God in the actualization of the world is a key component deserving of further exploration.

Philosophy

This study began with an examination of philosophical resources. While I am not a philosopher *per se*, I felt this to be an important starting point given the discussion about what it means to be human. Reflection on human subjectivity has some particular roots in Enlightenment philosophy, and my work here has but scratched the surface of its implications for theological study. In addition to Immanuel Kant, this project has found affinity in the philosophy of Alfred North Whitehead. Each thinker provides some key reflection on the world that aids the theological constructions that follow them.

Indeed the very relationship between theology and philosophy is something that merits further reflection. I have heard the simple statement that theology is like discerning a strikingly colorful butterfly moving through the air and the leaves, while philosophy is like taking that butterfly and pinning it to a black velvet cloth to examine its veins and coloring. While this statement reveals that it was made by a theologian who prefers to examine the butterfly in flight, the point it illumines is the way in which philosophy provides that sort of detailed observation of reality, while theology ebbs and flows like the flight of a butterfly, or even like Whitehead's description of the airplane in flight.

Philosophy and theology originate from and provide resource for different ways of viewing the world. Theologians must avail themselves of ways philosophers have engaged the world, and philosophers must reflect on the implications of theology for understanding the world. Both are a part of human intellectual life, and each is appropriate in its own way. I know that this book has only begun to engage the possibility of its philosophical resources.

Feminist Theology

From its original proponents, feminist theology has developed a character that has shifted and changed shape in the past forty years. Reconciling the original work of individuals like Valerie Saiving and Mary Daly with the present state of diverse "feminist" theological scholarship requires that we seek out the fundamental principles of what it means to be a feminist theologian in relationship with the Christian church. This book has not engaged feminist theologians outside the Christian church, and this area of interreligious dialogue is one rich with challenge and possibility.

The relationship of feminist theologies to the Christian "tradition" remains an unresolved tension. By virtue of its critical nature, feminist theology stands as a challenge to "business as usual" in the Christian church. At the same time, women who engage in feminist theology often themselves remain committed to some kind of life in the church. Why is this? Joanne Carlson Brown makes an analogy between the reasons that women give for staying "in" the church, and the reasons that women often give for staying "in" abusive relationships: I can make a difference in it—If I stay I can change it! It is for the good of the children. If I leave, where will I go? Really, it is good at the heart of it all.

Despite this scathing suggestion, women remain committed to doing theology within the parameters of the Christian tradition. For this reason, this project has attempted to engage figures such as Kant, Luther, Anselm, as well as contemporary theologians continuing in the line of "traditional" Christian theology. If we do not deal with them and their proposals, along with the good and the bad implications they have for theology from a feminist perspective, their power remains unchallenged and untested. The theology of Luther is not going to stop being an influence on my theology or on the Christian tradition as a whole, so I must engage it to engage its weaknesses and its strengths. In doing so, I maintain the connection to tradition that is an inevitable part of being in the human community.

The future of feminist theologies will be intriguing. For lack of a better word, I hesitate to predict anything about the future of feminist scholarship. I believe that diversities in sources, norms, and authorities will characterize future scholarship. I also hope that feminist theologians will not ignore or avoid engaging the "problematic" figures of the Christian past. This suggests that we maintain connection with historians who help us better understand the context within which these figures lived and wrote. In wrestling with them, we come out stronger and better theologians.

The Sacraments

This project has in some way framed some of the issues of the relationship between God and the human being in the manifestations of Christian theology seen in the sacraments. We drew from Luther's sacramental theology some of his presentation of the relationship, and we suggested that re-thinking atonement theory naturally leads to re-thinking sacramental theology. The moments of the sacraments serves as the sort of time and place location where we find many things expressed about God and affirmed about the human community.

I have limited the way in which we have spoken of the sacraments, and I believe that an adequate sacramental theology is yet to be developed from these insights. Certainly Luther's understanding of the sacraments involves more than his concepts of God and the human being, and the place of the sacraments within the life of the church today requires serious attention. I have approached the sacraments as a systematic theologian seeking to discern the ways that different aspects of theology come together to express something about the relationship between God and the human being. This is important insofar as it offers some theological reflection on which further scholarship and conversation can build. If we are to take some criticism of "traditional" constructions seriously, we must flesh out the ways reforming one aspect of theology affects other aspects.

This also should have some effect on the liturgy and the worship style that encompasses the sacraments. The sacraments are, after all, the heart of the worship life of Christians, and this book has not begun to address the implications for rethinking the sacrament of the eucharist for the rituals and the practices of our worship life. This is an area rich with resource and possibility.

The connection between the sacraments and the everyday lives of individuals is an area that is also rich with theological discussion. The brief mention of the series of articles by Martha Ellen Stortz on the sacraments and the social reform principles found in Luther does not do justice to the depth of their possibility. This conversation merits further attention, and it is my hope that such scholarship continues to enrich our theologies and our lives.

In Conclusion

Human life in the vision of God is characterized by commitment, mission, vision, risk, and struggle. It depends on the presence of God for vision and sustenance, and it works toward deeper actualizations of human agency and creative participation in the ongoing work of creation. It is revealed and destroyed through the life of Jesus as Christ, and it is resurrected by the power of God in the human community. Human life in the vision of God is difficult and it is beautiful. It is seen in participation in the eucharist, and it is actualized in every moment of existence. It brings responsibility and capability, and presumes a divine presence which lures the world toward fuller realizations of itself.

Bibliography

Abelard, Peter. "Exposition of the Epistle to the Romans (An Excerpt from the Second Book)." In *A Scholastic Miscellany: Anselm to Ockham*. Edited and translated by Edwin Rathbone Fairweather. Philadelphia: Westminster, 1961.
Althaus, Paul. *The Theology of Martin Luther*. Translated by Robert C. Schultz. Philadelphia: Fortress, 1966.
Anselm. "Cur Deus Homo." In *Basic Writings*. Translated by S. W. Deane. 2d. ed. LaSalle, Ill.: Open Court, 1962.
Aulén, Gustaf. *Christus Victor: An Historical Study of the Three Main Types of the Idea of the Atonement*. Translated by A. G. Hebert. New York: Macmillan, 1931, 1951.
Baker-Fletcher, Karen, and Garth Kasimu Baker-Fletcher. *My Sister, My Brother: Womanist and Xodus God-Talk*. Maryknoll, N.Y.: Orbis, 1997.
Bloomquist, Karen. "In Today's Context." In *The Promise of Lutheran Ethics*, edited by Karen L. Bloomquist and John R. Stumme. Minneapolis: Fortress, 1998.
Braaten, Carl E. and Robert W. Jenson, editors. *Union with Christ: The New Finnish Interpretation of Luther*. Grand Rapids: Eerdmans, 1998.
Brock, Rita Nakashima. *Journeys By Heart: A Christology of Erotic Power*. New York: Crossroad, 1988.
Brown, Joanne Carlson and Rebecca Parker. "For God So Loved the World?" In *Christianity, Patriarchy, and Abuse: A Feminist Critique,* edited by Joanne Carlson Brown and Carole R. Bohn. Cleveland: Pilgrim, 1989
Case-Winters, Anna. *God's Power: Traditional Understandings and Contemporary Challenges*. Louisville: Westminster John Knox, 1990.
Cobb, John B. Jr., and David Ray Griffin. *Process Theology: An Introductory Exposition*. Philadelphia: Westminster, 1976.
Daly, Mary. *Beyond God the Father: Toward a Philosophy of Women's Liberation*. Boston: Beacon, 1973.
———. *The Church and the Second Sex: With the Feminist Postchristian Introduction and New Archaic Afterwords by the Author*. Boston: Beacon, 1985.
———. *Pure Lust: Elemental Feminist Philosophy*. Boston: Beacon, 1984.
———. *Websters' First New Intergalactic Wickedary of the English Language*. Boston: Beacon, 1987.
Davaney, Sheila Greeve, editor. *Feminism and Process Thought: The Harvard Divinity School / Claremont Center for Process Studies Symposium Papers*. Symposium Series 6. Lewiston, N.Y.: Mellen, 1981.

Ebeling, Gerhard. *Luther: An Introduction to His Thought*. Translated by R. A. Wilson. Philadelphia: Fortress, 1964.

Edwards, Paul, editor. *The Encyclopedia of Philosophy*. 8 vols. New York: Macmillan, 1967.

Erickson, Millard. *Christian Theology*. 3 vols. Grand Rapids: Baker, 1983–85.

Ewing, A. C. *A Short Commentary on Kant's Critique of Pure Reason*. Chicago: University of Chicago Press, 1938.

Fairweather, Eugene R. "Incarnation and Atonement: An Anselmian Response to Aulén's *Christus Victor*." *CJT* 7 (1961) 167–75.

Farley, Wendy. *Tragic Vision and Divine Compassion: A Contemporary Theodicy*. Louisville: Westminster John Knox, 1990.

Fleming, William. *The Vocabulary of Philosophy: Mental, Moral, and Metaphysical*. New York: Sheldon, 1873.

Forde, Gerhard O. "The Work of Christ: Atonement as Actual Event." In *Christian Dogmatics*, vol. 2, edited by Carl E. Braaten and Robert W. Jenson. Philadelphia: Fortress, 1984.

Forell, George Wolfgang. *Faith Active In Love: An Investigation of the Principles Underlying Luther's Social Ethics*. New York: American, 1954.

Goldstein, Valerie Saiving. "The Human Situation: a Feminine View." *JR* 40 (1960) 100–112.

Gudorf, Christine. "The Power to Create: Sacraments and Men's Need to Birth." *Horizons* 14.2 (1987) 296–309.

Gunton, Colin. *The Actuality of Atonement: A Study of Metaphor, Rationality and the Christian Tradition*. Edinburgh: T. & T. Clark, 1988.

Harrison, Beverly. "The Power of Anger and the Work of Love." In *Making the Connections: Essays in Feminist Social Ethics*, edited by Carol S. Robb. Boston: Beacon, 1985.

Hefner, Philip. "Basic Elements of the Church's Life." In *Christian Dogmatics*, edited by Carl E. Braaten and Robert W. Jenson. Philadelphia: Fortress, 1984.

———. "Biocultural Evolution and the Created Co-Creator." *Dialog* 36 (1997) 197–205.

———. "The Cultural Significance of Jesus' Death as Sacrifice." *JR* (1980) 411–39.

———. "The Human Being." In *Christian Dogmatics*, edited by Carl E. Braaten and Robert W. Jenson. Philadelphia: Fortress, 1984.

———. *The Human Factor: Evolution, Culture, Religion*. Minneapolis: Fortress, 1993.

Isasi-Díaz, Ada María. "Elements of a Mujerista Anthropology." In *In the Embrace of God: Feminist Approaches to Theological Anthropology*, edited by Ann O'Hara Graff. Maryknoll, N.Y.: Orbis, 1995.

———. *En La Lucha, In the Struggle: Elaborating a Mujerista Theology—A Hispanic Women's Liberation Theology*. Minneapolis: Fortress, 1993.

Johnson, Elizabeth A. *She Who Is: The Mystery of God in Feminist Theological Discourse*. New York: Crossroad, 1992.

Kant, Immanuel. *The Critique of Pure Reason*. Translated by J. M. D. Meiklejohn. London: Bell & Sons, 1893.

———. "Foundations of the Metaphysics of Morals." (1785) Translated by Lewis White Beck. Englewood Cliffs: Prentice Hall, 1990.

———. "What is Enlightenment?" (1784) Translated by Lewis White Beck. Englewood Cliffs: Prentice Hall, 1990.

Keller, Catherine. *From a Broken Web: Separation, Sexism, and Self*. Boston: Beacon, 1986.

Kelsey, David H. "The Human Being." In *Christian Theology: An Introduction to Its Traditions and Tasks*, edited by Peter C. Hodgson and Robert H. King. Philadelphia: Fortress, 1982, 1985.

Kemp, John. *The Philosophy of Kant*. London: Oxford University Press, 1968.

Lorde, Audre. *Sister Outsider: Essays and Speeches*. Trumansburg, N.Y.: Crossing, 1996.

Luther, Martin. *Luther's Works*. 55 vols. Edited by Jaroslav Pelikan and Helmut T. Lehmann. Philadelphia: Muhlenberg [Fortress], 1960, and St. Louis: Concordia, 1959.

———. *D. Martin Luthers Werke. Kritische Gesammtausgabe*. Weimar: Bohlau, 1884.

Megill-Cobbler, Thelma. "A Feminist Rethinking of Punishment Imagery in Atonement." *Dialog* 35 (1996) 14–20.

Noddings, Nel. *Women and Evil*. Berkeley: University of California Press, 1989.

Oberman, Heiko. *Luther: Man between God and the Devil*. Translated by Eileen Walliser-Schwarzbart. New Haven: Yale University Press, 1989.

———. *Luther: Mensch zwischen Gott und Teufel*. Berlin: Severin und Siedler, 1983.

Pannenberg, Wolfhart. *Anthropology in Theological Perspective*. Translated by Matthew J. O'Connell. Philadelphia: Westminster, 1985.

Pederson, Ann. *Where in the World is God?: Variations on a Theme*. St. Louis: Chalice, 1998.

Pero, Albert and Ambrose Moyo, eds. *Theology and Black Experience: The Lutheran Heritage Interpreted By African and African-American Theologians*. Minneapolis: Augsburg, 1988.

Peters, Ted. "The Atonement in Anselm and Luther, Second Thoughts about Gustaf Aulén's *Christus Victor*." *LQ* 24 (1972) 301–14.

Peura, Simo. *Mehr als ein Mensch? Die Vergöttlichung as Thema der Theologie Martin Luthers von* 1513–1519. Veröffentlichungen des Instituts für Europäische Geschichte Mainz, vol. 152. Mainz: von Zaubern, 1994.

Ray, Darby Kathleen. *Deceiving the Devil: Atonement, Abuse, and Ransom*. Cleveland: Pilgrim, 1998.

Ross, Susan A. *Extravagant Affections: A Feminist Sacramental Theology*. New York: Continuum, 1998.

Runes, Dagobert D., editor. *The Dictionary of Philosophy*. New York: Philosophical Library, 1942.

Russell, Letty M., and J. Shannon Clarkson, editors. *Dictionary of Feminist Theologies*. Louisville: Westminster John Knox, 1996.

Solberg, Mary. *Compelling Knowledge: A Feminist Proposal for an Epistemology of the Cross*. New York: SUNY Press, 1997.

Sponheim, Paul. *Faith and the Other: A Relational Theology*. Minneapolis: Fortress, 1993.

Stortz, Martha Ellen. " 'The Curtain Only Rises': Assisted Death and the Practice of Baptism." *CTM* 26 (1999) 4–18.

———. "'Practicing what it means': Welfare Reform and the Lord's Supper." *CTM* 26 (1999) 19–32.

Suchocki, Marjorie Hewitt. *The Fall to Violence: Original Sin in Relational Theology*. 1994. Reprinted, Eugene, Ore.: Wipf and Stock, 2003.

———. *God–Christ–Church: A Practical Guide to Process Theology*. New York: Crossroad: 1982, 1989.

Tambasco, Anthony J. *A Theology of Atonement and Paul's Vision of Christianity*. Collegeville, Minn.: Liturgical, 1991.

Teselle, Eugene. "Atonement." In *A New Handbook of Christian Theology*, edited by Donald W. Musser and Joseph L. Price. Nashville: Abingdon, 1992.

Theissen, Gerd. *Biblical Faith: An Evolutionary Approach*. Translated by John Bowden. Philadelphia: Fortress, 1984.

Trelstad, Marit. "Relationality Plus Individuality: The Value of Creative Self Agency." *Dialog* 38 (1999) 193–98.

VanDyk, Leanne. "Do Theories of Atonement Foster Abuse?" *Dialog* 35 (1996) 21–25.

Walker, Alice. *In Search of Our Mothers' Gardens*. New York: Harcourt Brace Jovanovich, 1983.

Whitehead, Alfred North. *Adventures of Ideas*. 1933. Reprinted, New York: Free Press, 1961.

———. *The Function of Reason*. Boston: Beacon, 1929, 1958.
———. *Modes of Thought*. New York: Macmillan, 1966.
———. *Process and Reality: An Essay in Cosmology*. New York: Macmillan, 1976.
Williams, Delores S. *Sisters in the Wilderness: The Challenge of Womanist God-Talk*. Maryknoll, N.Y.: Orbis, 1993.
Wink, Walter. *Engaging the Powers: Discernment and Resistance in a World of Domination*. Minneapolis: Fortress, 1992.

www.ingramcontent.com/pod-product-compliance
Lightning Source LLC
Chambersburg PA
CBHW071502150426
43191CB00009B/1401